Dorothy Stapleton

Quirky Quilts

CONTENTS

Introduction p2

CHAPTER 1
CRAZY QUILTING p6

Crazy patchwork p8
Quilt: *I Hate Housework*
Projects: kitchen wall-hangings

Embellishing p12
Quilt: *The Housewive's Lot*
Project: exotic evening bag

Machine Embroidery p17
Quilt: *What Is?*
Project: Alice's playmat

The Envelope Method p20
Quilt: *Why*
Project: child's placemat

New Designs from Old p24
Quilt: *It's Not All Hearts and Flowers*
Project: anniversary hanging

CHAPTER 2
LOG CABIN p30

The Basic Techniques p32

Log Cabin Houses p36
Quilts: *A Veritable Coronation Street!*
Project: house cushion cover

Folded Log Cabin p40
Quilts: *You've Been Framed*
Project: log cabin picture frame

Curved Log Cabin p42
Quilt: *Land of the Long White Cloud*
Project: sheep may safely graze

Log Cabin Combinations p46

Liberated Log Cabin p48
Quilt: *A Night at the Opera*
Project: Ben Bates' quilt

CHAPTER 3
FUN WITH FABRIC p52

Machine Quilting p54

Using Bleach p56
Quilt: *Blue Lagoon*
Project: gentleman's comforter

Black on Black p60
Quilt: *The Sailor's Return*
Project: flower-basket cushion

Hammered Leaves and Flowers p64
Quilt: *Take Time to Smell the Flowers*
Project: nettle mirror-frame

The Basic Boring Bits p69

Acknowledgements p72

Welcome to... Quirky Quilts

I have always loved working with my hands. I was considerably younger than my three sisters and so was brought up as a child in an adult household. My big sister Marjorie was very influential on my upbringing: she was at art school, and always asked me to pose while she sketched me – she also taught me to knit, sew and generally be creative. Being the baby of the family also had a down side: I can remember being hauled out from lunch by my mother and given a good smacking for showing off. What a change: now I get paid for showing off in public.

I was packed off to a boarding school when I was seven. It was good fun at first, in the sort of Enid Blyton–Mallory Towers–school stories way. There was so much free time to fill and amuse yourself in; no home comforts such as television, or snuggling up by the fire with a book on a comfy sofa. Therefore, I started to make things. I was a great fan of kits: marquetry, painting-by-numbers, jewellery created out of plastic wire, making glass vases with old sweet papers stuck to the back, flowers from crepe paper. My poor family had to accept these efforts as presents.

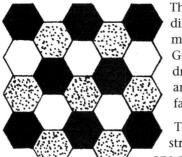

Then, when I was about 12, I discovered patchwork and made my first quilt. My Grandma and Aunt had a drapers' shop before the war and they had kept bits of fabric, which I was duly given.

The quilt turned out rather strangely as I didn't realise that one couldn't make a hexagon quilt from panne velvet and chiffon mixed with cottons. I cut out the hexagon shape

from old Christmas cards. First mistake: it was an octagon. Maths has never been my strong point. This meant that I had to keep adding small squares to make it possible to join the patches together.

I brought the quilt home in the holidays and worked on it daily. I found my Five-Year Diary recently, the sort little girls had with a lock and key to record daring and exciting deeds to be kept from their mothers. Mine was rather sad. 'Did patchwork, took the dog for a walk.' My life hasn't changed that much, except now I haven't even got a dog. I did finish the quilt, slightly cheating as I added a huge frill around the edge to make it fit the bed.

I was one of the brave girls at school who actually took needlework for GCE. The teacher was very fierce and we spent many hours practising machining with a treadle machine on paper before we were allowed to progress to fabric. We had flat irons (I'm not that old: it was just an old-fashioned school…) I still shudder at the thought of the sleeve I put in back to front, having not paid attention to the instructions: I had the sound of 'You're deaf as well as daft, are you?' ringing in my ears.

I decided to go to art school when I left school and thought theatre design would be fascinating. It promised: dress design, set painting and an exciting career. When I got there I found the department was staffed by men in pink mohair stoles wearing silk racing colours: this was rather alien to me, straight from my all-girls boarding school (this was the unenlightened 1950s). So I made a snap decision to study pottery, as the teachers were bearded men in Aran sweaters.

After a couple of years I realised a four-year course in Industrial Pottery wasn't my thing. We had to make 26 identical teapots to get the perfect one. The first one was exciting, except when I rushed home with it proudly to use for tea, and found it wouldn't pour as I'd forgotten to make the holes in the spout.

The culmination of the course was a month in Stoke on Trent in January. It was cold: I missed home and my boyfriend. I slept in my duffel coat, as the digs they allotted us had a hole in the window. So on my return my then boyfriend, and now long-suffering husband of 35 years, suggested we got married.

Once we were married I had my three sons fairly quickly, so chose to find a career to fit in with my family. Adult craft teaching was ideal; hours to suit, nice people, lots of girlie gossip, and a constant challenge to learn new things to pass on. First I taught painting, then batik and tie-dye, then macramé (this *was* the 60s, remember...), then eventually patchwork.

I then met my good friend Linda Tudor; she offered me a share in a craft market stall in Covent Garden. We made cushions and small quilts; we actually sold quite a lot of things, but it was a financial disaster as the next stall was a jeweller, so if we made a sale we then spent it on new earrings. Also it was so cold in the winter that expensive coffee and pastries ate into the profits. It was fun meeting the public; one lady bought a big floor cushion on her way to the opera – she said it wasn't a problem: she would sit on it.

I then had a lucky break. One of our products was a cathedral window cushion; we had devised a different way of doing cathedral window using a cardboard template and exploding the sides out to make an interesting shape. I took a cushion-front up to John Lewis, a large London department store, to get a zip. While I was waiting to pay the supervisor came over and commented on what a pretty and unusual cushion it was. When I said I had made it she asked if I would make an appointment with the buyer and supply them with cushion covers. So we then started a cottage industry, making cushions for London shops and then quilts for Liberty's in London.

It worked really well when the boys were small (between Linda and me we have five boys); we packed ourselves up kits to work on, and then sewed together three times a week. Eventually we went our own ways creatively, she becoming an embroiderer and me carrying on the continuing obsession with patchwork and quilting.

Why do I love patchwork? I think it's got something to do with the fact that I'm incredibly thrifty (some might say mean). I can't bear waste. I'm the sort of person who saves small bits of food in the fridge then insists on eating them all up even though I know they will be dried up and disgusting. So to me the idea of cutting up old clothes or using waste products actually to create something useful and nice to look at is just wonderful. As to how I began to evolve my Quirky Quilts – well, read on!

How it all began...

In 1987 I had started entering the national patchwork competitions: it gave me a deadline to finish something, and I felt it also made me try and strive for a better finish, knowing that the public would be looking for wobbly edges and bad stitches! It was the time when all quilters seemed to be getting involved with 'designer fabrics': there was a mood around that if you were making quilts out of old clothes in the 'make do and mend' tradition it was sort of inferior. The National Patchwork Championships had a recycled category and I decided to enter by making a quilt from the contents of my kitchen drawer.

This was the first crazy quilt I had made, and I wanted it to be in the tradition of Victorian crazy quilts. I knew the technique from looking at old quilts in books and in Worthing Museum. There was a slight snag: I only knew two stitches – lazy daisy and herringbone, which I had used for turning up skirt hems (the herringbone, not the lazy daisy, I'm not that silly). A friend, Linda Tudor who I mentioned earlier, came to the rescue and taught me new stitches as I went along.

I made each block on a backing of old flannelette sheet, and used: yellow dusters, drying-up cloths, table napkins, washing labels, J-cloths (brightly-coloured bonded cotton cleaning cloths), and a table napkin from the Ritz Hotel in London. (I'm not a kleptomaniac: one of my nieces had her wedding reception there and we were given some cake wrapped in it.) It's a lovely pink colour and seemed to go well with the blues and greens of the cleaning cloths and the vivid yellow dusters. As it had *The Ritz* embroidered on it, I added 'I'd rather be at' in front: this started a trend in my quilts which I still can't seem to stop, adding silly embroidered quips.

I then decided to call it *I Hate Housework,* and added lots of sayings, some in common usage but most made up like:

✎ **Only spring clean when Granny's due to visit**

✎ **Cobwebs are an art form**

✎ **Be creative – make a mess**

✎ **Save the ozone layer – don't use polish**

✎ **Why don't moths eat bits of cotton on the carpet**

✎ **On the day of judgement will they count the quilts or the polished floors?**

✎ **Dust preserves the furniture**

The binding is made from old kitchen curtains from a jumble sale plus table napkins, and the back is teatowels. Truly recycled. The finished quilt is 36in (92cm) square. It won an award of merit at the National Patchwork Championships and the cup for humour at Quilts UK, so I got the feeling that other people sympathised with the sentiments! You can see the finished quilt on page 9: appropriately, I've used it as the basis for the first projects in the book.

Where it's gone since

Since then I've gone on developing many of the ideas, themes and techniques that I used in *I Hate Housework*. The slogans and little quips have become one of the features of my quirky quilts, and people seem to enjoy reading them – I even see people surreptitiously writing them down at quilt shows! To save you smuggling notebooks into shows, I've included some of the slogans from the quilts in this book. Recently I've been trying out the writing in bleach on a coloured background – see page 57 for more on using bleach.

I've also continued to use crazy patchwork in quite a few of my quilts; some of them are stitched by hand (see *The Housewive's Lot* on page 12), and some are stitched by machine, which opens up all kinds of possibilities (see *What Is?* and the playmat on page 17). Crazy patchwork has a long history of being embellished with beads, flowers, sequins, buttons etc, and I've continued and developed that tradition by adding more and more items that I collect from different places – the shells from New Zealand in *Land of the Long White Cloud* (see page 42), and things I literally found around the house in *Learning to Love Housework* (featured on the front cover).

The first section of the book covers different ways of using and developing crazy patchwork.

As well as my crazy quilts, I've created all kinds of different quilts and pictures with variations of the log cabin technique – there are so many ways of using log cabin that I've devoted a whole section of the book to it. And, ever keen to try new ideas, I've included a section on one-off techniques – interesting and intriguing ideas that you may not have tried before.

Why I've written this book

When I'm demonstrating at quilt shows or giving talks to groups, I'm constantly being asked why I haven't written a book. I've always felt that my quilts were very personal to me, and so wouldn't translate well into a 'how to do it' book, but Gail and Chris Lawther convinced me that by describing my quilts, and then having similar projects to make, it would work. Also, I felt that this way it could keep a light-hearted feel which reflects my style.

I'm rather unorthodox in my choice of fabrics, choosing to make quilts from dishcloths and other bizarre things, but I love sharing techniques which I have picked up or developed. Recently I made a video on the log cabin technique, showing the basics then going beyond these to make pictures, and my feedback has been that quilters enjoy making these slightly quirky quilts.

All my quirky quilts were exhibited at the Spring Quilt Fairs in 1998; you will also find details with each quilt of other places it has been shown, such as NPC (National Patchwork Championships) and EQC (European Quilt Championships).

I hope that you'll find reading this book like looking at my quilts: I hope it will intrigue you, inform you, but most of all that it will bring a smile to your face. The nicest compliment I've ever had about a quilt was when two ladies at a show came up to me and said they had to make a dash for the loo as they had laughed so much!

Dorothy

How the book works

The book's divided into three chapters: **Crazy Quilting, Log Cabin** and **Fun with Fabric**. Each chapter contains several sections, with each section introducing a different technique – for instance, how to do crazy patchwork by machine, or how to create house and garden designs out of log cabin blocks.

Every technique features one or more of my own quilts as inspiration, and also contains a smaller project which you can do or adapt yourself if you want to try the technique out.

At the very back of the book you'll find all the basic boring bits, such as how to make a quilt 'sandwich' and how make up a cushion cover, plus how to do some of the embroidery stitches for crazy patchwork and some of the other techniques mentioned in the projects. You'll also find a list of people who have helped me out in putting this book together, and stockists for some of the more specialised materials.

So all that's left is for you to dip into *Quirky Quilts* – enjoy the book.

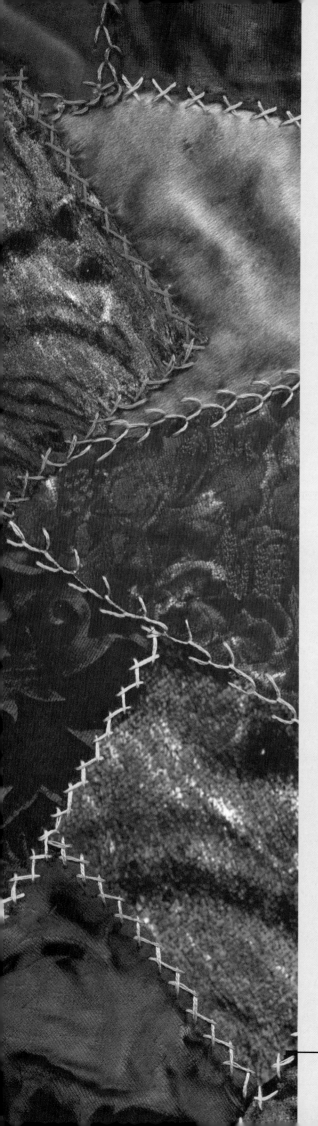

CHAPTER 1
Crazy Quilting

Crazy patchwork is the name given to a method of piecing odd-shaped scraps of fabric into a random design: there's no formal pattern or layout – anything goes. The earliest examples of crazy patchwork were probably not deliberate – perhaps a hard-up homemaker cobbling odd pieces of leftover fabric into a patch to cover a hole in a garment or a bedspread – but the formal version of the technique came into full flower in Victorian times.

The Victorians loved to decorate everything in sight, even piano legs, and this was also an era when time-consuming hobbies were sought to while away the hours – what a change from nowadays, when we're all trying to fit our creative hobbies in with a thousand and one other jobs! As leisured Victorian ladies would have their clothes made for them by a dressmaker there were many scraps around to be used: crazy patchwork was the perfect answer.

Victorian crazy patchwork used silks, satins, brocades and velvets, overlapping them in a random pattern on a backing fabric then covering the raw edges with lavish embroidery stitches – see the detail of Worthing Museum's Jubilee Quilt above, made in 1887-8. The stitches sealed the raw edges, attached the patches to the backing fabric and showed off the embroidery skills of the ladies.

The colours of the fabrics were usually very rich – dark blues, deep greens, reds and black – and the stitching was generally worked in vivid colours of twisted silk. The embroidery stitches are traditionally herringbone or feather stitch on the raw edges of the patches, and motifs or pictures were often added to the centres of the patches in satin stitch, sometimes with beads and sequins incorporated as well (just in case the piece wasn't quite ornate enough…).

In this section I'll show you some of the different ways I've used variations of crazy patchwork in my quilts, along with a project or two for each technique which will give you a chance to try it out for yourself.

Crazy patchwork

Forget the satins and the velvets: based on my *I Hate Housework* quilt, these crazy projects make use of dusters, cleaning cloths and washing labels, but are pieced or embroidered in the traditional way.

Embellishing

You don't have to stop at embroidery: send your crazy patchwork projects really over the top with added buttons, beads, flowers and sequins, and produce some sumptuous evening bags along the way.

Machine embroidery

Take the crazy out of crazy patchwork: let the machine take the strain, and use it for all the fiddly stitching. Run up a bright play-mat like the one below with bits from your scrap-bag.

Envelope method

An ingenious way of getting rid of all the raw edges, which I developed for a quilt that used up all my unfinished pieces from workshops. The technique can be adapted to create projects small and large.

New designs from old

Add a zaniness to traditional patchwork patterns by replacing some of the patches with crazy piecing – rediscover some old favourites, and make some new friends. This is a great way of using up bits and pieces of fabric that are too small to be used for conventional patchwork!

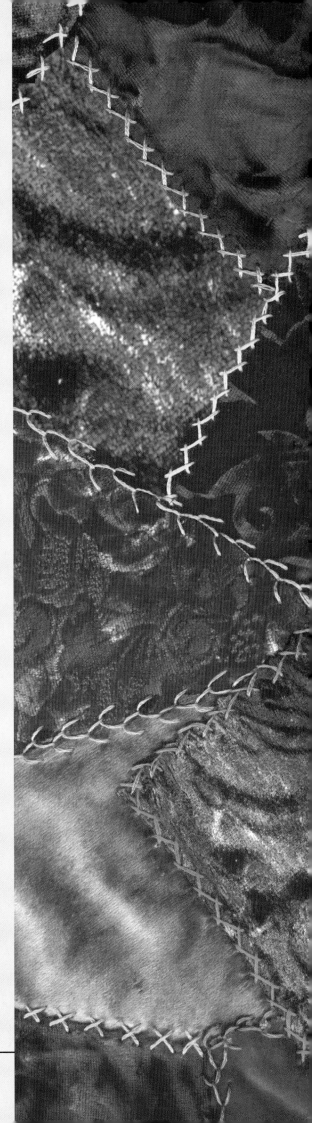

Crazy Patchwork

Traditional crazy patchwork is stitched by hand, using overlapping patches of exotic fabrics stitched in place with decorative hand embroidery. Using this technique, the Victorian stitchers – sometimes male, but usually female – made table runners, tea cosies and sofa throws as well as cushions and bags. These objects weren't quilted, as they were already pretty thick, but backed to conceal the underside of the embroidery stitches, and some of the items such as tablecloths had ornate ruched or fringed borders added. It's a technique you either love or hate: some people find the fussiness overpowering. I saw it described in a 1950s embroidery book as 'the supreme efflorescence of tastelessness' – now there's a title for a quilt.

In this section we update the technique – same idea, but using materials that are quintessentially 20th century! The main quilt opposite is the first of my quirky quilts, (see the story of how it came about on page 4), and I've developed two kitchen wall-hangings picking up the kitchen/housework themes.

THE QUILT
I Hate Housework

1987
36x36ins (92x92cm)

Award of Merit NPC
1st prize for humour and 3rd prize for small wallhangings
Quilts UK
Made In Britain exhibition, San Diego

This quilt of all the quilts I've made has struck a chord with people: they all love the sentiments – although I once met a lady who said she loved housework. It subsequently won the cup for humour at Quilts UK, and has been exhibited many times including being part of a show in America.

The hands holding the top are made from household gloves; I toyed with the idea of rubber gloves but thought that was going too far, even for me. These are cotton gloves which I think you're meant to wear for dirty jobs like cleaning the silver – a lady once told me her husband used them for cleaning his motor bike. I stuffed them with wadding and applied them to the top, with the fingers making a V sign and with a wooden thimble sewn on to one finger.

This aspect of the quilt has caused some problems as, because the fingers are sticking out, it's difficult to roll the quilt. I was giving a talk recently and waiting in a multi-use hall. A man from a chess group walked by and asked what I was doing: when I said that I was waiting to give a talk to the quilt ladies, he asked 'Are you a conjurer?' I was rather taken aback, but he explained he thought I had rabbit's ears poking out of the top of my bag… it was the two fingers.

PROJECT 1
There's more to life than housework

I've included two projects on this theme: one is a small one-block hanging like *I Hate Housework,* made with dusters and cleaning cloths etc, and one is an appliqué made solely with bonded cleaning cloths (like J-cloths). These could be hung on the kitchen wall; if you get inspired you could make several similar blocks and sash them them with strips of a plain fabric, like my large one, for a bigger quilt or hanging.

A word about the materials: yellow dusters run when washed, so if you think you'll ever want to wash the hanging, wash the dusters first. Bonded cleaning cloths come in various patterns and colours according to the supermarket. Either swap with friends or have your own cleaning cloth stash; your family will find it more acceptable than that huge stash of patchwork fabric awaiting a rainy day…at least the cleaning cloths are useful.

✦ **MATERIALS**
for a 12in (31cm) hanging
✧ 12in (31cm) square of calico (or waste fabric such as an old teatowel)
✧ 14in (36cm) square of dark fabric for the backing (this will be brought round to the front to form the binding)

- ❖ An assortment of dusters, bonded cleaning cloths, teatowels, old table napkins etc
- ❖ Fabric washing labels from garments
- ❖ Anchor stranded embroidery threads in bright colours
- ❖ Any motifs cut from suitable fabric (cakes, jars, fruit etc), backed with Bondaweb and cut out. These are useful for covering up awkward fraying bits!
- ❖ 6 or more shirt buttons
- ❖ Pigma pen or water-soluble/fading pen
- ❖ Curtain ring (optional)
- ❖ Ordinary Sylko sewing threads

✦ METHOD

1 Cut a 12in (31cm) square from the calico or waste fabric.

2 Cut random shapes from the dusters and cleaning cloths: try and vary the sizes and shapes. The dusters have a distinctive red stitched edge, so try and use that, and the corners have a nice curve. The bonded cloths don't fray and so are very useful for butting up to and overlapping pieces that might fray. Old table napkins usually have a nice finished edge which can be used to great effect.

3 Position your pieces on the background square and play around with them until you get a pleasing arrangement. Remember that you'll want to write some slogans on the hanging, so make sure there are some plain areas big enough to take the writing. This is the kind of occasion when a 'door spy' comes in useful. These are the little spy holes that are in front doors to see if undesirables are outside; you can get them easily and cheaply from hardware stores. If you look through it at your work it makes everything recede into the distance, and colours or shapes which are obviously wrong shout out to be changed. It's like when you see a photograph of a quilt: patterns appear which you sometimes hadn't noticed in the actual quilt.

When you are happy with the colour and shape balance pin the pieces to the backing, making sure the cleaning cloths are overlapping any dusters which are more liable to fray. Tack the pieces down so that they don't move during the hand embroidery, or machine them down with a toning thread.

4 Now for the fun bit! Cover all the raw edges with embroidery stitches in stranded cotton to enhance the shapes and hold the patches in place; use nice bright colours, and vary the colours and stitches across the piece. Herringbone, blanket stitch and feather stitch (see page 71) all work well and are in the tradition of crazy patchwork; there are many other embroidery stitches which could also be used, and many books showing them. The edges of the non-fray cloths can be anchored down with lazy daisy stitches (see page 71) or large cross stitches in stranded cotton.

5 Take another critical look and then add appropriate Bondawebbed pieces to cover up any nasty joins. (You can also use the buttons later to cover up small awkward spots – see stage 7).

6 Find a plain space on a piece of duster or napkin and write your slogan or slogans: use some of mine (see page 4), or make up your own. Write with a Pigma pen or washable felt pen, then cover this with backstitch in two strands of embroidery cotton.

7 Check the edges and then trim if necessary to 12in (31cm) square. Position this square centrally on the dark 14in (36cm) background square, so that there is an even border all round, and pin in place. (As there are many layers of fabric I haven't used a wadding for this project, but you could add a piece between the top and backing if you wanted extra thickness.)

Now add the shirt buttons, either to cover up nasty joins or spaced so that they hold the top layer to the bottom.

Fold the backing fabric to the front in a double hem to make a binding and hem it down. If you are a bit worried about not having neat mitres at the corners, add four more buttons to cover the evidence! (It's amazing how many ways you can improve your quilts by cheating slightly.)

Make a small casing on the back of the square for hanging, or attach a curtain ring at a corner and hang the square on point.

☞ **TIP**

For a more random effect, bind the edges of your hanging with strips of cleaning cloth in different colours – as I've done in the photograph on page 9.

PROJECT 2
Washing flowers

This little hanging is made solely from bonded cleaning cloths. (Well, now I've made you buy them in so many different colours you've got to use them up…). The flowers are made from layered shapes and applied with shirt buttons. The teapot is made from a bonded cloth in a different colour or pattern from the others used.

✦ MATERIALS
- ✧ Dark fabric for background, 10x15in (25x38 cm)
- ✧ Backing of a brighter fabric, 12x17in (31x43cm) (this will be brought round to the front to form the binding)
- ✧ 2oz wadding, 10x15in (25x38cm)
- ✧ Bonded cleaning cloths in blue, pink, yellow, orange, green
- ✧ Pearl-type shirt buttons
- ✧ Anchor stranded embroidery cotton in green, yellow, red and orange

✦ METHOD
1 Cut your own freehand flowers from 2in (5cm) squares of cleaning cloth, or trace or photocopy the flower shapes on this page and use them as templates. Vary the colours you use, but save one colour exclusively for the teapot.

2 Cut some thin strips of green cleaning cloth for the stems, and cut large and small leaves using the patterns below.

3 Trace the teapot shape below onto your remaining cleaning cloth and cut it out. Pin the teapot onto the background and 'arrange' the flowers and leaves in it; again, take time to make sure you're happy with the arrangement, then pin the pieces in place.

4 Using three strands of red stranded cotton, work blanket stitch around the teapot as shown on page 71. This is intended to give it a naive, rustic look, so the stitches can be nice and big. Stitch the stems and leaves with the green thread using tacking-size running stitches. Finally, appliqué the flowers by sewing a button in the middle – these can all be sewn with yellow or orange thread, or with a mixture of colours. Make some of the flowers 'doubles' by putting two shapes on top of each other.

5 Make a 'sandwich' (see page 70) with your top, wadding and backing, making sure that there is an even border of the backing fabric all around. Tack the layers together, or pin them with safety pins. Fold the backing fabric to the front in a double hem to make a binding and hem it down. You can then add hand-quilted flowers or contour quilting, or machine quilt a few flowers in a pretty pattern as described on page 55.

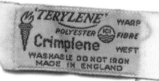

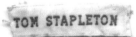

Embellishing

E mbellishing is the technique of adding decorative stitches and actual objects to the surface of the quilt. I used to be a purist and found it rather distasteful to have embellishment on quilts, thinking of quilts as useful, utilitarian items. Then I started making wall-hangings and became a convert, and like all converts I have now taken to this technique with gusto. A few years ago I went to a contemporary exhibition at The American Museum in Bath, and was bowled over by the vibrancy of the quilts decorated with added buttons and sequins and badges.

THE QUILT

The Housewive's Lot

1996
54x68in (137x173cm)
1st prize for embellishing, NPC

THE HOUSEWIVE'S LOT SLOGANS!

✎ He has a night out at the RSC (Royal Shakespeare Company) She has a night out at the PTA (Parent Teachers Association)

✎ He reads Penguin books, She reads Pingu Books (a children's book character)

✎ He lunches with the Architects, She lunches with the Archers (a midday radio soap opera)

✎ He sees Picasso's Blue Period, She sees Blue Peter (a children's TV programme)

This quilt is a size I find very useful, as not only is it a reasonable size to work on – not too large for machining – but it just covers the crack in my dining room wall! You may think it would be easier to fill and paint the crack: yes, but it's not as much fun as making a quilt to disguise it.

In the 1960s there was a women's magazine called *Nova*; each month they published poems by an American author, Judith Viorst, under the title *'It's Hard to be Hip and Over 30 and Other Tragedies of Married Life'*. (Now there's a title for a quilt!) One of the pieces was called *Where is it written?* It just touched a nerve, as at the time I had two children under two, was living in a crumbling Edwardian house that was being lovingly and slowly renovated, and was also trying to run the local playgroup.

I 'filed' the poem in the kitchen drawer and years later unearthed it. It has lines like: 'Where is it written that husbands get ego gratification, emotional support, and hot tea in bed for ten days when they have the sniffles, while wives get to give it to them.' And: 'Where is it written that husbands get to meet beautiful lady lawyers and beautiful lady professors of ancient history and beautiful sculptresses and heiresses and poetesses, while wives get to meet the checker with acne at Safeway.'

I had had teatowels printed with my *I Hate Housework* slogans and was toying with the idea of having an apron printed. (I then remembered the disruption of having 500 teatowels clogging up my small hall and decided against it.) Aprons were therefore in my mind. I find with crazy patchwork it can be very muddled if there isn't a positive image or shape in a plain colour to rest the eye. For instance, in *I Hate Housework* the sashing works as the foil: in *Why* it's the Y shapes

themselves. Therefore my shape for this quilt was to be an apron.

I searched in vain through my plain fabrics to find a piece large enough to cut into an apron shape. I then had the inspiration: why not use a real apron? So I bought a plain blue one, which had the added advantage of the pockets to fill with items.

I used man-made insulated curtain lining for the wadding. This is available from curtain shops; it's fairly inexpensive, and it's slightly sticky – the fabric adheres to it like a children's Fuzzy Felt kit. I had the backing fabric and the curtain lining, then placed the apron centrally and tacked it down. I then added my crazy pieced fabrics. The pockets were filled with J-cloths, dusters, a teddy bear, a shopping list. (It's a family joke that no-one can understand my lists as I have my own shorthand).

There are two wooden spoons made from some wood-effect fabric, and a piece of shirting with a designer label. This was another family tale. My sister gave me a tartan cotton skirt, but as she is slimmer and taller than me it didn't fit. So, waste not want not; I cut it up. Horror! When I got to the waistband I saw the label: Ralph Lauren. So as not too feel too profligate at chopping up designer gear I used the label on this quilt, and the fabric in a wedding quilt for my nephew.

I just love unusual and bizarre fabric, and on this quilt I managed to find some corkers. My penpal in America sent me the Right and Wrong Way to Eat a Banana fabric (top right). I can always rely on Barrie Trickett (the other man in all quilting ladies' lives!), who as Tritex sells some wonderful wacky fabric like the Thunderbirds and cricketer stuff. The Kilner and jam jar prints, and the cutlery fabric, were from my local fabric shop.

Of course as usual I used the cleaning cloths as well.

I embellished the quilt with hand stitchery (as shown on page 71), and with fancy stitches on my sewing machine (see page 17). I also stitched on buttons, washing labels from clothes and some Alexandra roses. I added a row of safety pins above the pocket, including an old-fashioned nappy pin. When my sons were babies I used to look down at my chest while queuing in the supermarket and find I still had a nappy pin stuck to my jumper. I also pinned on a note, the sort you leave on the kitchen table for the family who haven't turned up for supper: 'Your supper's in the dog love Mum'.

The whole apron shape was herringbone stitched to the backing in orange stranded cotton, with the pocket outlined and the apron strings folded up at an angle to give a decorative effect. I quilted the whole piece by machine with transparent thread in free wiggly patterns to hold it together. The male and female signs were quilted in blue and pink stranded cotton; all the slogans I wrote in crayon and then backstitched with yellow thread.

Most of these are *not* a dig at my husband, who is saintly at putting up with all my mess and fabrics, but the Jaeger one is true. He had two pairs of grey cord trousers: gardening ones and Jaeger ones. I muddled them up, and put the Jaeger ones in the wash on a hot programme. They shrunk and were then also demoted to gardening trousers. When I made the quilt I thought, 'I'll snip out that label and use it'. As it was in the back pocket I just cut off the entire pocket, and of course forgot to tell him. He, poor thing, put his secateurs in his back pocket and they promptly fell down into his wellington boots. Who'd marry a quilter?

PROJECT
Exotic evening bag

I'm indebted to Linda Tudor, my great friend, for the pattern of this bag. She made me one for a wedding and it's big enough to hold makeup etc and even a small camera. The strap is just the right length so that the bag fits comfortably under the arm for the dreadful reception balancing act of drink, plate, canapé etc.

◆ MATERIALS
◇ Foundation fabric (calico or waste fabric) 10x7in (25.5x18cm)
◇ Strips of various velvet, silk or sparkly fabrics at least 2in (5cm) wide and 7in (18cm) long. These can be in toning colours or a random assortment.
◇ Pelmet Vilene 15in (38cm) square
◇ Lining fabric 15in (38cm) square
◇ Bag backing fabric 13x7in (33x18cm); this will fold over the top and be visible so must tone with the patchwork
◇ Assortment of lace, fine ribbon. buttons, fabric flowers, trinkets and spangles to decorate
◇ 45in (115cm) of silk or cotton bias binding in a toning or contrasting colour
◇ Bondaweb 15in (38cm) square
◇ Ribbon(s) for the strap

◆ METHOD
1 Enlarge the patterns on page 15 to the correct size, either by photocopying or drawing, then use shape A as a template to cut a piece from the calico and the lining. Use shape B to cut a piece from the backing fabric and the lining.

2 Select strips of the silks and velvets and machine them across the calico bag front at a slight angle in a flip and sew method (see page 72). Lace can be added on top of a contrast strip or as an edging. When the calico is covered, trim the edges back to the original size of the pattern.

3 Now the fun bit: decorate with the fancy stitches on your machine, using various coloured threads including metallics. Add trims of lace, or thread ribbon through larger lace pieces. (I found some tatting from my late mother-in-law's sewing box). I also added some lampshade edging. You can add trinkets, spangles, buttons, beads or fabric flowers, or even create your own embroidered flowers – in fact, just go over the top! The more you do, the better it works.

4 Cut a piece of Vilene to match the shape of the decorated section and iron it to the wrong side to stiffen it. Fuse the matching piece of lining to the Vilene using Bondaweb. Stiffen the wrong side of the piece of backing fabric with Vilene, Bondaweb and lining fabric in the same way.

5 Seal the straight top edge of the bag front with bias binding. I find it easier to do this by hand as by now the bag is rather stiff for machining.

6 Pin the two pieces wrong sides together and secure them with zigzag stitching round the matching edges, leaving 1in (2.5cm) open at the top of the sides for fixing the handle and edging the top flap.

7 Cut 2 ½in (6cm) of fine ribbon or silk tape for the fastening and sew it firmly to the point of the flap in a loop. Seal the flap with the binding, making a small pleat where the loop is. This can be covered by a button or a spangle if you want to disguise the join!

8 Use rounded velvet ribbon or plait several fine coloured ribbons to make a handle approx 36in (92cm) long; sew the ends firmly to the top edges of each side of the bag.

9 Bind the entire remaining edge, sewing by hand with a matching thread. You could machine the binding with a fancy stitch in contrasting cotton if you want a snazzier effect. Go out on the razzle and await the compliments.

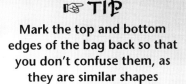

☞ **TIP**
Mark the top and bottom edges of the bag back so that you don't confuse them, as they are similar shapes

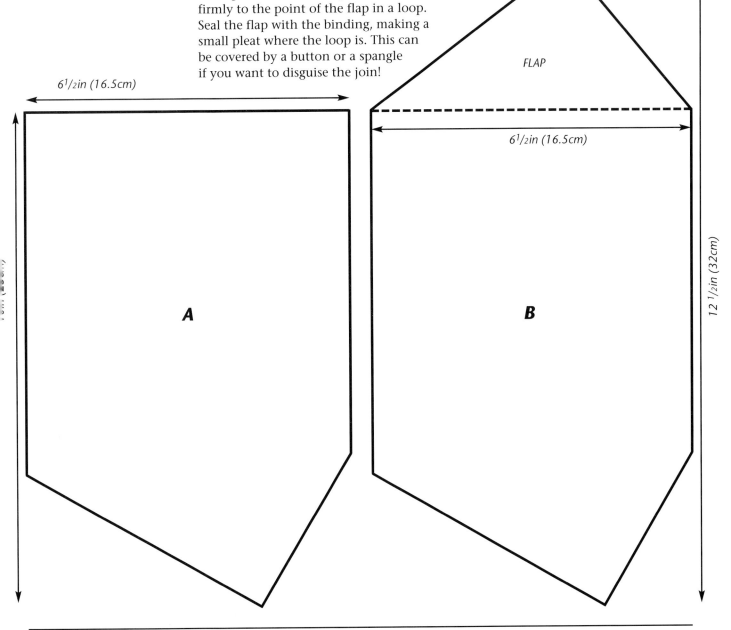

6½in (16.5cm)

A

FLAP

B

6½in (16.5cm)

12½in (32cm)

EMBELLISHMENTS

As well as decorative stitching by hand and machine, there are all kinds of different things that you can use to embellish your quilt.

☞ CHARMS AND TRINKETS

There are now little trinkets and charms sold specially for quilts and embroideries, such as tiny scissors and thimbles. Many of these are made of metal, but you may also find some fun ones in plastic or resin.

☞ BUTTONS

These come in all kinds of shapes and sizes, and some are designed to look like real objects such as pencils, footprints, butterflies, birds and animals (remember the ladybird buttons on the children's pyjamas?!) Large shops stock whole ranges of exciting buttons in an astonishing variety of colours, sizes and finishes, and there are speciality shops and mail order catalogues exclusively for buttons (see the stockist list on page 72).

Most families have a button tin: do you remember those happy hours while Mum was doing the mending, rooting through it to find buttons to thread into a necklace? Charity shops often have a sweet jar full of buttons which they are happy for you to sift through. Old shirts have a double use: the fabric for piecing or foundation backings, and the pearl buttons. Shirts with button-down collars have dinky little ones for the purpose. Buttons are useful not only as a decorative feature but can also cover up some tricky joins. You can also use them for 'quilting' the layers of a quilt. They can be applied in many decorative ways, as you can see above.

☞ BEADS

Different kinds of beads can be used to catch the light and to add sparkle and texture to a quilt; they can also be applied to particular areas of the fabric as part of the design. Like buttons, beads can also be an anchoring method to keep the layers of a quilt together, and once again they are available in a wide variety of shapes, colours and finishes and have their own exclusive stockists (see page 72).

☞ FABRIC FLOWERS

Flowers add an old-fashioned charm to a quilt. It's possible to buy silk flowered tape by the yard, and individual little silk flowers are also available (I used them on the Wedding section of *It's Not Always Hearts and Flowers*). Another option is the fabric flowers sold for charity flag days. I have used the pretty pink Alexandra roses, which are made from cotton fabric the same as the better-quality poppies; having removed the yellow plastic stamen bit, they look good combined with surface stitchery, as in *The Housewive's Lot* (see page 12) and the evening bag project in this section.

☞ RIBBONS

Ribbons are available in a myriad colours and widths. The very fine ones are particularly useful for embellishing, and you can even do embroidery stitches with them. The Victorians made whole log cabin quilts from hat ribbons, so nothing's new. Tiny narrow ribbon bows are also available from specialist shops and from the haberdashery departments of large stores; these add a lovely touch to embellished quilts.

Machine Embroidery

As my quilts tend to be made in a crazy way, adding many layers and not using regular shapes, this can make hand quilting difficult because of the bulk of fabrics. A while ago I began to experiment with machine quilting and found that, with the feed dogs down and using a darning foot, I could quilt in free shapes and even draw pictures with my needle. On pages 54-55 I describe how to do some of the more pictorial effects that you can achieve with machine quilting: for this quilt and project, though, I just used fancy stitches on my sewing machine.

One very effective method of machine quilting is to find a scalloped machine stitch and then make it maximum width; it looks very dramatic. Try out some machine embroidery stitches made wider, and experiment. These effects also work well with some of the variegated threads available for machines these days: this adds to the random, crazy effect of the whole quilt.

THE QUILT
What Is?

1995
40x51in (102x130cm)
NPC
Cornish Crafts Exhibition

We were trying to by a new car – well actually a second-hand car. When we read the small ads they seemed totally incomprehensible. When we asked a friend what FSH meant and found it was Full Service History, I became interested in acronyms. First I thought I might work on some things that men would understand, like ABS (advanced braking system), and ones for women like HRT (hormone replacement therapy). I abandoned this as being too difficult, and so muddled the acronyms up somewhat. I actually picked one up from a TV play: it was WOM (wife's own money).

I made the quilt in nine blocks of 10x14in (25x36cm); the finished quilt measures 40x52in (102x132cm). I started with some very small scrap pieces and applied them onto a backing fabric using the full repertoire of all the machine embroidery stitches on my machine, so the effect is a sort of colour wash. The edges of the fabric are raw, but the stitches prevent them from fraying.

As I mentioned on page 13, crazy quilts need a positive plain image to organise the chaos. This time I chose a question mark. I cut several question mark shapes out and applied them with one of the fancy stitches. Disaster! They went all puckered and looked awful. I'm afraid I hate unpicking and always try and bodge up a mistake, so I hit on the idea of trapunto. This is a very old embroidery technique of stuffing the work from the rear to make a padded effect. I decided to make small holes in my question marks and poke in fluffed-up wadding, using a knitting needle.

Second problem: big hole showing – so why not make a big feature of it and cover it with an embroidered flower? When I sashed the quilt in black, third problem: the blocks looked just slightly out of alignment, and being black, showed up in contrast to the busy coloured blocks. Oh well, add more flowers on each corner: the edge is softened and the misalignment isn't noticeable.

I machine-quilted the entire piece with bright rainbow thread by selecting an automatic scalloped stitch on my machine and turning the stitch width to the widest possible setting: it creates a lovely curved pattern. The last block of the quilt says RSVP, ASAP, PTO (please reply, as soon as possible, please turn over). The reverse of the quilt has question marks applied and the answers embroidered onto them. The fancy stitches had come through to the back, making a nice all-over pattern.

Next problem in a continuing series: people aren't allowed to look at the backs of quilts in shows without the say-so of the white glove ladies (known as 'quilt angels' in America). I exhibited this quilt, though, at The Cornish Crafts Association gallery and they asked if there were any special requirements, and it was hung sideways on so that people could walk around it and read.

THE PROJECT
Alice's playmat

This is a quilt for a baby or toddler which is put on the floor so that he or she can lie safely on it to kick and play. (The same design could easily be worked in different fabrics for a picnic rug.) By using lots of images like cars, teddies and ducks, it makes it a learning aid too: a sort of picture book to lie on. The first one I made was for my granddaughter Claudia, who lives in Australia where it's too hot to have a cot quilt and where sitting-room floors tend to be ceramic – rather hard for little ones to lie on and play. That one was so bright that people said I would have to send her sunglasses to use it. Amazingly, in the bright light out there it looked quite subdued.

✦ **MATERIALS**
for a 40x58in (102x147cm) mat
✧ Backing fabric 44x62in (112x158cm); this is larger than the front so that it can fold over as the binding. If you want to use this as a snuggly use a brushed cotton fabric. Pick a dark colour as it's going on the floor.
✧ 40x58in (102x147cm) of either man-made insulated curtain lining (as page 13), or 2oz polyester wadding
✧ Various scraps of childish and bright fabrics. This can include printed blocks with houses or animals on them, strips of fabric with ducks etc. These are usually in the bargain bins at shows!

❖ Rainbow machine thread, or many different coloured Sylko threads.

◆ **METHOD**

1 Cut the wadding to size and place on the backing fabric so that there is a 2in (5cm) border all round.

2 Starting with larger pieces, possibly a printed block, place pieces randomly on the wadding. Remember to place them at angles and overlapping in places. If you are using images like trains, cars, teddies etc, make sure they are not all facing the same way. Pin the pieces down.

3 Use your automatic machine stitches if you have them, or a small zigzag if you don't, and stitch the patches in place using the rainbow thread. If you find it too bulky, do half the quilt at a time. Make sure there aren't any little gaps in the stitches, because if there are those little fingers will surely find them and might get caught.

4 Iron Bondaweb behind any printed images on fabric which you want to cut out and apply.

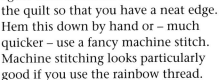

These can then be stitched on with the fancy stitches. This method

takes lots of bobbin thread, so buy the very large reels of thread – or make a feature of using all those different-coloured bobbins threaded and never used. It will make the back look very jolly...

5 Fold the raw edges of the backing fabric to the front by 1in (2.5cm) all the way around the quilt and iron; fold them over again onto the front of the quilt so that you have a neat edge. Hem this down by hand or – much quicker – use a fancy machine stitch. Machine stitching looks particularly good if you use the rainbow thread.

6 Remember to embroider 'love from grandma' on the back.

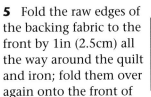

The Envelope Method

This is a method of constructing a quilt where each block is completely finished (like a table mat) before they are joined together. I first came across it when Pilgrim Quilters, the group to which I belong, made a group quilt in this way as a leaving present for one of our founder members. Anyone who's tried to assemble a group quilt will know of the amazing poetic licence people have with the given block sizes! This method is good for group quilts as the discrepancies in size can be dealt with more easily than with traditional techniques.

The block is sewn in the same kind of way that you would construct something like a pillowcase, with seams around three sides. The front, back and wadding are all cut to the same size, then the back and front are put wrong sides together, with the wadding on top, machined round three edges, then turned right side out and finished. I used the method for my quilt *Why*, shown on the right, and I've used just one envelope to make the table mat shown with my hungry grand-daughter, Zoë, below.

THE QUILT

Why

1993
51x49in (130x125cm)

1st for humour, Quilts UK
2nd for recycling NPC
Made in Britain Exhibition,
San Diego

This was the second quirky quilt I made. Having chopped up the contents of my kitchen drawer to make *I Hate Housework* I decided to attack my sewing room drawer. I go to workshops on various methods and friends teach me things, but somehow I never even finish the samples, let alone the quilt. They get put away for that day when I will have the time and the inclination to finish them, which is never. What a joy to cut them up and assemble them into a crazy quilt knowing I never have to finish the samples. I wanted to put writing on it again: I don't know why I love writing on my quilts, as I can't spell and it's very time-consuming hand embroidering all the words.

The theme of the quilt was 'Why did I …' etc. It was looking rather a muddle and as I was puzzling over it walking to the postbox it suddenly clicked that a large Y on each block would tie it all together. A lot of quilting is thinking

✎ 'Why not sew something useful' (cut-out dress shapes intended for a cot quilt)

✎ 'Why can't I sew a straight line and I still like log cabin' (a particularly wonky discarded piece)

✎ 'Why do I always make one extra block and leave it in the drawer for 5 years' (an extra block from a quilt about The Great Storm of 1987)

✎ 'Why did I lose the pattern' (a workshop in USA with the lady who bought my house quilt)

'Why did I buy this fabric' (from my collection of horrendous fabric, with Superman on it)

'Why do I go through the rubbish bin' (a block assembled from the cut-off bits out of the rubbish bin)

'Why am I so mean I save shop samples' (made from tiny samples of fabric)

'Why do I never finish things' (samples from a Christmas workshop)

'Why are stripes so hard to use' (from my stash of striped shirting)

'Why is stained glass so hard' (from a workshop, with the tacking still left in the bias strips)

time, which isn't better than counting sheep in the night as it gets the old brain whirring and sleep is even harder, but I do often get my best ideas at strange times.

I planned it to be 18 blocks – six across and three down. I cut them out, and blow me down; when I came to assemble it I had made one block too many – I had 19. So I added it to the bottom as a PS with 'Why am I so stupid I've still got one left'. This is a standing joke with my friend Linda, that I always have a starter kit for the next quilt with the bits left over from the last one.

I then needed to sash the quilt as it was far too 'busy' and needed a calming influence to break up all the pattern. This proved a slight problem. As I had made the blocks in the envelope method I had to do the sashing likewise. This is a bright turquoise fabric: I laid out my blocks and made 3in (7cm) strips of a front, back and wadding as before. I

machine quilted this in straight lines and cut it to fit the blocks. I then herringbone stitched the blocks to the sashing both on the front and the back. I have never seen a quilt assembled like this and I began to see why! I managed to pin it to my ironing board to keep it taut while I sewed. It actually hangs remarkably straight.

I always have a problem with my quilts hanging well, partly because I have often added everything but the kitchen sink so maybe I expect too much. The problem is that it is the last job to put on the hanging channel and then – horror – it looks wonky. I did get over this problem with stretching the quilt as you would a tapestry. Spray the quilt with water from a squirty bottle till it is slightly damp, then pin taut to a carpet in a room you're not using and leave for a few days. The result is amazing. My *Mediterranean Sunset* quilt (see the sides of pages 30 and 31) was so distorted that John suggested I take a tuck in the side! I was nearly in tears, having spent months hand quilting, let alone piecing, the thousands of minute log cabin strips. It was due to be exhibited at Edinburgh Art Gallery the next week. It stretched out fine and has remained so, so give it a try.

Each block in *Why* has a different fabric on the back, and I put a label on each as to whose workshop the bits were from. Maybe I'll now be on a workshop black list. As well as going in shows in this country it's been exhibited in the USA; currently it hangs in my hall.

THE PROJECT
Child's placemat

☞ TIP

This is a lifestyle tip. We all want to spend all our time sewing, but if you make up lots of home-made soup and large casseroles and freeze them, your family will be so impressed they will forgive the cotton all over the floor.

This is very easy to make; the front is a piece of bright children's fabric with the knife, fork, spoon and plate appliquéd on the top. You could embroider some pertinent writing on the plate.

- *Eat up, there's a good boy/girl*
- *Yum Yum*
- *It looks scrummy Mummy*
- *Eat up your greens like Popeye*
  Or for older people:
- *Not as good as my Mum made*
- *Not lamb again*
- *It looked better in the book*

I'm sure you can think up some sayings for your own family. I know President Bush of America had some choice words about broccoli! My family used to have some awful mealtime rhyme about who finished the meal first: 'First the worst, second the best, third's the one with the hairy chest!' This always caused tears from the third, I can't think why.

✦ MATERIALS
for a 12x16in (31x41cm) mat
- ✧ Bright cotton print, 13x17in (33x43cm)
- ✧ Wadding or dolmette the same size
- ✧ Backing fabric the same size
- ✧ Contrasting cotton fabric for the cutlery and plate
- ✧ Toning Sylko sewing thread
- ✧ Tracing paper
- ✧ Anchor stranded cotton in a colour to contrast with the plate

✦ METHOD

1 Make a sandwich of the bright fabric face up, the backing face down, and the wadding on top. Pin the layers together, and machine around three sides with 1/2in (1.5cm) seam allowance; leave one short side open for turning. This now looks like a pillowcase.

2 Clip across the corners, and turn to the right side. You might need to poke a crochet hook or a pencil into the corner to get a nice point. Press well, turning in the seam allowance on the open edge. Topstitch by machine all round the mat, just in from the edges.

3 Trace the pattern for the knife, fork and spoon onto the tracing paper and cut out. (Or, if you prefer, photocopy the shapes). Draw round a plate or saucer approx 6 1/2in (16.5cm) diameter and make a tracing paper pattern from this.

4 Cut these shapes from the contrasting fabric and iron a few strips of Bondaweb on the back. Fuse the pieces in position on the front of the bright fabric as in the photograph, then machine stitch round the edges with a fancy stitch or zigzag. This 'quilts' the layers of the mat together.

5 Write on your chosen saying with either light-coloured crayon or hardened soap. Embroider with backstitch using three strands of embroidery cotton.

You can also make excellent table mats by covering rectangles of calico with strips of fabric using the flip and sew method (see page 71). Choose fabrics that complement your dining room, and cut them in strips of different widths. When each rectangle is covered, finish in the way described above.

New Designs from Old

Traditional patchwork patterns can easily be adapted for crazy patchwork by substituting crazy piecing for some of the patches that make up the design. I've used this method for the large Double Wedding Ring quilt and the smaller anniversary quilt shown in opposite. It's best to create the crazy pieces on a foundation of scrap fabric first, and then assemble the pieced sections onto a further foundation fabric as if they were a jigsaw puzzle – this saves piecing bulky seams. The pieces are tacked into position, then the raw edges covered with fancy stitching by hand or machine – I've used embroidery in stranded cotton.

THE QUILT

It's Not All Hearts and Flowers

1993
49in (125cm) square

Finalist MASQ competition 'New Quilts from Old Favorites'
Exhibited Paducah
Cup for humour Quilts UK

♥ **The Romance:**
It was all hearts and flowers
Is he too old – he's 21?

♥ **The Wedding:**
They thought we were too young
Why does a nice girl like you
want to marry our son? (said to
me by my mother-in-law)

♥ **The Children:**
Why Mummy, why, why, why
Why does Lego multiply on the
carpet?

♥ **The Advice:**
Keep a sense of humour
Never cook his supper till
you've seen the whites of
his eyes (said to me by the
wife of one of my
husband's colleagues)

♥ **The Niggles:**
Kleenex in the wash
Why weren't new men
invented in 1963?

I first used this method in my quilt *It's Not all Hearts and Flowers*. I wanted to make a quilt as a present for my husband for our 30th wedding anniversary, and Double Wedding Ring seemed the obvious choice of pattern. I also wanted it to have crazy piecing and to have silly sayings about marriage written on it. The Double Wedding Ring pattern has a nice graphic quality about it; sometimes it looks like intertwining circles, and it can also look like large petal shapes.

I cut out the curves for the rings in a foundation fabric, old flannelette sheet. (I seem to be always acquiring friends' and elderly parents' throw-outs. If you keep things long enough you'll eventually find a use for them. I did think that old crimplene skirts were beyond the pale, threw them away, then found they would have been very good for rag rugs.) I applied my crazy pieces to the foundation by flipping and sewing (see page 72); this meant that there weren't any raw edges to worry about. Each circle depicts a different stage of marriage, so I tried to match the fabrics to the subject of that circle: pretty flowery fabric for the romance and wedding, children's fabrics for their section, and household fabrics and washing cloths for that section etc.

I then applied the pieced sections directly to the backing and wadding. I used a cotton wadding, which seems to adhere to the fabrics and makes it easier to work.

This left me with gaps to fill: the petal shapes created where the rings overlap, and the central curved squares. I could then 'cheat' by cutting these patches out quite roughly and tucking them under the curves. (If you do Double Wedding Ring conventionally it's quite a difficult piecing problem as

you have to join convex and concave curves, so this seemed a good deal easier.)

For the next stage I tacked the entire quilt, and covered all the raw edges with close herringbone stitch in various coloured threads. I embellished it with buttons, ribbons and a flag day flower (as page 16.) The buttons helped to anchor down the curved sections, and the plain sections I hand-quilted heavily in self-coloured thread.

Then for the sayings. I mentioned to some quilting friends that I was doing a quilt with sayings about marriage, and one kindly sent me some very erudite poetry quotations. I think she was rather taken aback when she saw my idea of marriage quotations...The quilt is in nine sections, so I added nine sets of writing: I wrote the words with slivers of hardened soap, then backstitched them in stranded embroidery cotton.

The sayings about the teenagers were really from the heart. I've definitely done my time on that score. Having three boys I've had:

☆ changing a left-hand-drive car to right-hand in the driveway, making an oil-slick larger than the Torrey Canyon. I actually have a friend, the mother of girls, who didn't know what Swarfega was (in case you're in the same happy state, it's green, grease-removing jelly).

☆ Playing guitars and drums in the bedroom at all hours.

☆ Going for a day's windsurfing at 10am, returning at 4am, omitting to tell me he was going on to a party, when I had already rung the coastguard to enquire on drownings and planned his entire funeral.

☆ Playing the hi-fi so loud that the vibrations knocked off one of my wooden decoy ducks. They then stuck its head back on the wrong way

♥ **The House:**
There's more to life than housework
Is DIY hereditary?
(I think it is: my son managed to drill through his wall into next door)

♥ **The Teenagers:**
We don't like pop, raves, smoking and motor bikes
They don't like Mozart, family parties, sherry and early nights

♥ **The Departures:**
You'll miss them when they've gone (granny's favourite remark)
Why are they fit to live with when they're living with someone else? (I saw a similar sentiment on an anniversary card and thought how very true it was)

♥ **The Peace:**
Two of us again
He must be a saint putting up with me for 30 years.

round. I may have never noticed if it had been done properly.
☆ Kidding me that the plants growing on his windowsill were actually tomatoes!
☆ Temporarily becoming a Buddhist and chanting loudly for two hours at a time in his non-soundproof bedroom.

But I've been lucky; we've never had:
- the police
- hard drugs
- body piercing.

Now they really *are* fit to live with: new men who change nappies, cook meals, enquire after their mum, and visit bearing flowers and bottles of wine. When we visited my son in Australia, we went out to dinner, came back at 11.30 to find the door locked and the house in darkness: he came to the door and said 'what time of night do you think this is!' How times have changed.

Back to the quilt. I cut the corners off and bound the whole quilt edge. I belong to The American Quilters Society, and read in their magazine that they were having a competition called New Quilts From Old Favorites. Each year they take a traditional design, then choose 18 quilts which have used the pattern in an innovative manner. That year the subject was Double Wedding Ring. It seemed such a coincidence, so I sent a slide of my quilt, never thinking it would be chosen as it

was a world-wide competition. Amazingly I got a letter saying I was a finalist and they would like the quilt sent for exhibition at the Museum of the American Quilters Society (MAQS). I then read the rules: the quilt had to be a minimum size of 40in (102cm). I measured mine: it was 4in (10cm) too small. I toyed with the idea of sending it hoping they would think our measurements are different in England, then I thought I must resolve the problem.

I had called the quilt *It's Not All Hearts and Flowers* because of a lovely letter an old aunt of my husband's had written us when her husband died. She said 'we had a very happy life together but it wasn't all hearts and flowers'. So I got some printed heart fabric, the sort that comes in strips, backed the strips with fabric and stuffed them with teased-out wadding. I then found some crewel-work embroidered pieces which I got years ago from a jumble sale – they looked as if they might have once decorated a 1930s cardigan, and had been 'filed' on my notice-board. I backed them with fabric and neatened the edges with buttonhole stitch, then I applied them onto each chopped-off corner and the effect was great. It made the quilt just the right size, and also improved it immensely, giving it a sort of old-fashioned look that was just right for its title. It subsequently travelled round the USA for a further two years, so poor John was rather late getting his present.

THE PROJECT
Anniversary hanging

This is a smaller version of my quilt using four rings – you can of course make it into a larger hanging or a quilt. I've made mine as a Ruby Wedding hanging (35 years), but you could have a Silver Wedding (25 years) or a Golden Wedding (50 years), using fabric coloured to suit the occasion. It could also be a wedding hanging, with the bride's and groom's names plus the date of the wedding; the signatures of the family members could be embroidered on the plain areas, in the tradition of the old signature quilts which were often made by church groups.

The fabric in the crazy pieced segments can reflect the interests of the couple. I have used fabric with wind-surfers, lighthouses, horses and music.

✦ **MATERIALS**
for a hanging approx 30x30ins (76x76cm)
✧ four pieces of plain fabric 10in (26cm) square for the curved squares

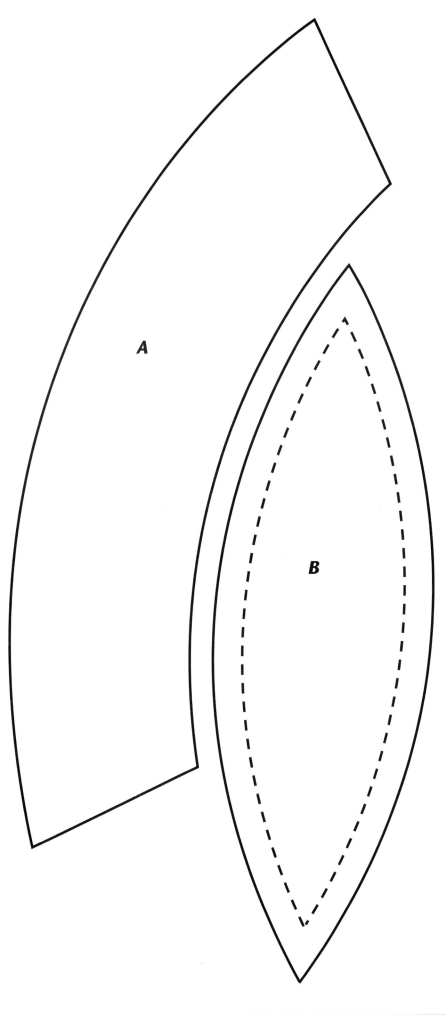

A

B

◇ 12 pieces of a darker toning fabric, 8x2¹/₂ins (20x65cm), for the lozenge shapes. [This will take a piece of fabric approximately 8x39ins(20x99cm)]
◇ Large piece of calico or a waste fabric for backing the curves
◇ Nine 4in (10cm) squares of calico
◇ A selection of scrap fabrics in appropriate patterns for covering the curves
◇ 36 2in (5cm) squares of various fabrics
◇ Backing fabric 30in (76cm) square
◇ Cotton wadding, dolmette or synthetic curtain interfacing 30in (76cm) square
◇ Anchor stranded cotton in a bright contrasting colour
◇ Sylko quilting thread in a toning colour
◇ 4¹/₂yd (4m) of cotton or silk bias binding

✦ METHOD

1 Trace round the patterns on the left.

2 Use pattern A as a template to trace and cut 24 curves in calico.

3 Cut strips of scrap fabrics in varying widths, and machine these onto the curves in a flip and sew method as shown on page 72. Make sure each curve is completely covered, then press the piecing well and trim each section back to the original shape of the curve.

4 Cut 13 lozenge shapes (using pattern B) in the darker fabric. (I've used velvet to give some texture).

5 Lay the backing fabric on a flat surface; cover with the wadding or interlining, and smooth the layers out well. Using the top diagram on page 29 as a guide, arrange the curved shapes onto the wadding (this is when the curtain interfacing is good as the pieces seem to stick onto it easily). You will have square sections left around the edges and in the centre: these are filled later.

6 The gaps left between the pairs of curves make the lozenge shapes: slip those pieces under the curves. The large gaps remaining are the central curved squares; slip the four large fabric squares into position under the curves. Pin and tack down all the pieces.

7 Hand quilt 'in the ditch' (just next to the seam) all the small segments making up the curves; this then holds the whole thing in place.

8 Using two strands of stranded cotton in a nice bright contrasting colour, work herringbone stitch round all the raw edges apart from the very outside of the shape – these will be bound later.

9 Cover each 4in (10cm) calico square with with four of the 2in (5cm) squares of fabric – use four different patches for each piece of calico. Fuse these on with Bondaweb and then herringbone-stitch over the raw edges. (If you think this is all too much fiddle, just use 4in (10cm) squares in a contrasting colour instead.) Position the squares to fill the eight gaps left around the edge of the quilt and the one in the middle.

10 Bind the entire edge with the bias binding, either by hand or by machine.

11 Mark the relevant names, dates etc in crayon or hardened soap, then backstitch them using stranded cotton. If you wish, embellish the quilt with heart-shaped buttons or trinkets appropriate to the occasion.

Note: I've made my hanging by hand but you can easily make it by machine using zigzag or those embroidery stitches on your machine instead of herringbone stitch. You can also embellish your quilt – on my large quilt I used some of the jumble-sale embroidered pieces like the one below.

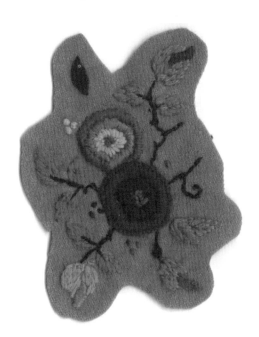

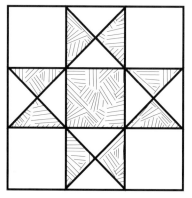

Ohio Star

Many traditional blocks designs can be adapted for crazy patchwork by replacing some of the areas with crazy piecing. Make a new fabric by flip-and-sewing (see page 72) randomly cut scraps onto a backing fabric, then cut these out exactly to size, with no seam allowance. The non-crazy pieces are also cut exactly to size and then assembled onto a further backing piece like a jigsaw puzzle, bonded or tacked down (to avoid bulky seams), and then embellished with hand or machine embroidery. This would make a very rich throw or a great cushion cover.

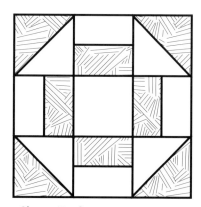

Churn Dash

Basic Nine-Patch

Shoofly

Card Trick

NEW DESIGNS FROM OLD

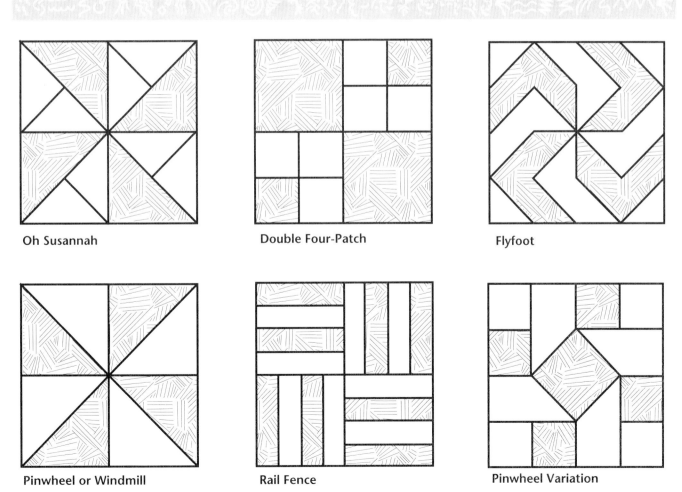

Oh Susannah

Double Four-Patch

Flyfoot

Pinwheel or Windmill

Rail Fence

Pinwheel Variation

CHAPTER 2
Log Cabin

og cabin is a very old patchwork pattern – there are even mummy wrappings in the British Museum which use the log cabin technique. It quickly became a popular design as it only requires small strips and therefore was ideal for recycling old clothes and dressmaking scraps. There are examples from the 1880s made from hat ribbons. The technique can be worked on a backing fabric so that even fabrics that are usually unsuitable for patchwork, such as sheers and loosely-woven cottons and wools, can be incorporated.

The name of the pattern derives from the early American settlers' log houses. According to tradition the central square is red to signify the fire in the hearth, the light strips suggest the glow from the fire and the dark strips the shadows.

There are two basic blocks: the spiral, using light strips on one side and dark strips on the other, and courthouse steps, in which the strips are added to opposite sides alternately giving the effect of a flight of steps. It helps to keep the strips of light fabrics and the strips of dark fabrics in separate bags at the beginning of a project – then you can just dip your hand in and select the most suitable fabric.

I became obsessed with the possibilities of log cabin years ago, and continue to experiment with it. The main reason is that there are no templates – and it really does use up all those tiny scraps. My first double bed quilt was a log cabin: I made it quilt-as-you-go in browns and blues (another continuing passion of mine). I read in a book that a traditional wadding was old blankets, so being pathologically mean I cut up a threadbare blanket for my wadding. It was lovely to quilt, but the finished quilt is so heavy it stops the circulation in your legs! It came in useful though when one of my sons was at college in North Wales.

That was in 1982, and I have always had some log cabin project on the go ever since. In this section of the book I'll show you how to create the basic log cabin blocks, and then various ways in which you can use them to create all kinds of pictures, patterns and landscapes.

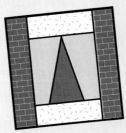

The basic techniques

Just what it says – how to create the spiral, courthouse steps, and other ways of stitching the basic log cabin blocks. All the techniques needed for the projects in this section.

Log cabin houses

Design your own street of houses, perhaps embellished with trees and a flower garden. This can either be a small cushion or hanging, or if you're feeling ambitious you can quilt Coronation Street!

Folded log cabin

An ingenious method which makes use of folded strips of fabric to produce a fabric photograph frame. Stitch the strips in place, then simply tuck the photograph under the folds.

Curved log cabin

Log cabin landscapes don't have to be limited to houses: stitch your own pastoral scene of sheep grazing on an idyllic hillside, or turn several curved log cabin blocks into stars.

Log cabin combinations

Combine basic log cabin blocks in different ways to create secondary designs – from Barn Raising to Streak O' Lightning.

Liberated log cabin

Take the measuring out of log cabin: set it free by combining it with crazy patchwork to create free-form blocks that can be built up into quilts. Use fun fabrics like the block here, or try the exotic silks and metallics I've used for *A Night at the Opera* for a really over-the-top effect.

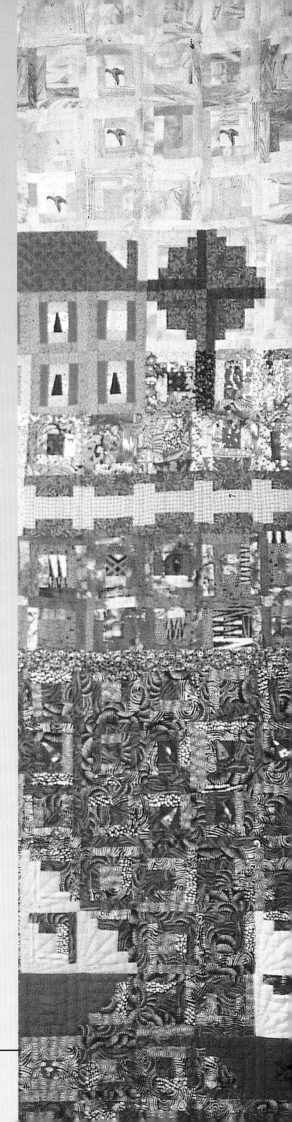

Log Cabin – the basic techniques

As I mentioned in the introduction to this section, there are two basic blocks used in the different log cabin designs: these are the spiral, and courthouse steps. All the other techniques – curved log cabin, liberated log cabin, house and garden designs etc – are variations and combinations of these two blocks.

Whichever basic block you are using, each design begins with a central square: the size of the square depends on the effect you want to achieve, and occasionally I'll give you instructions for a larger square than usual for a particular project. If you're new to log cabin, though, begin here with the basics and start by using a 1in (2.5cm) central square and edging it with one-inch strips in light and dark fabrics.

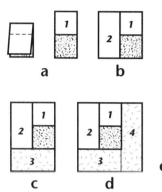

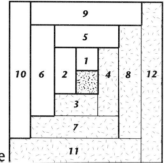

☞ TIP

It can be muddling at first to know which strip is the next one to be pieced. I've devised a little foolproof method. After the first round look at the block edges. One edge has no seams, two have one seam, but one edge has two seams on it: that's the one which will have the next piece added to it.

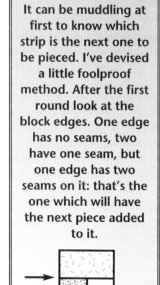

THE SPIRAL

a *Place a light strip face down on the central square, edges matching. Machine 1/4in (6mm) from the edge, using the machine foot as the guide. Trim the strip to fit the square and press outwards.*

b *In the same way, stitch the second light strip down the side of the square and the first strip; trim the strip to fit and press it outwards.*

c *Continuing to work your way round the central square, sew a third strip – a dark one this time – to the side of the square and the second strip.*

d *Sew the fourth strip (dark) to the edge created by strip 3, the square and strip 1 to complete the first round.*

e *Continue adding light and dark strips until the block is the required size. The numbers on the block show the order in which they are added – you can see that you just continue working your way around the square in a spiral (hence the name!).*

Note that the last strip of every round extends over the whole side of that round. The strips can be graded from light to dark within each side, but take care not to use the same fabric as a medium-tone in both the dark and the light sides.

COURTHOUSE STEPS

This is a much easier method of construction – that's why it's second, in case you wouldn't want to learn the spiral! The effect of the steps is created by piecing the lights and the darks in a different order from the spiral: they are sewn to the top and bottom of the central square first, and then to the sides.

a *Join a light strip to the central square, just as for the first step of the spiral design.*

b *Sew the second light strip to the opposite side of the square.*

c *Sew strip three (dark) onto the right-hand side, so that you join it to the edges of the square and strips one and two.*

d *Sew strip four (dark) opposite strip three.*

e *Continue adding strips on opposite sides, light at the top and bottom and dark at the sides, until the block is the required size.*

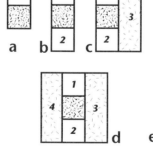

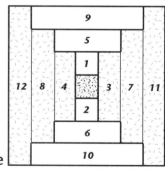

CORNER LOG CABIN

In this design, used to build up some pictorial blocks such as Butterfly, the strips are only added to two sides of the square instead of to all four.

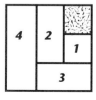

LOG CABIN HOUSES

You can create wonderful houses, gardens, trees, boats and landscapes using different log cabin blocks. Here are instructions for basic window, door, roof, garden and tree blocks – you can put these together to your heart's content to create whole streets of dwellings, or build them into the cushion cover shown on page 37.

Window block (A)

a *Begin with a dark central fabric square (if the lights are off!) or a pale yellow one (lights on). Curtains are added from scrap fabric: use a very small print so that it looks realistic. Cut one scrap and place it face down diagonally on the square; machine a straight seam.*

b *Turn back the piece and press. Add a second piece on the other side in the same way, then trim back to the size of the original square and measure it for accuracy. If you prefer a blind on your window, just sew a strip of lace across the top (see diagram) and continue in the same way.*

c *Using the courthouse steps method of construction, sew strips 1 and 2 in the lintel fabric to the window.*

d *Add strips 3 and 4 in brick fabric.*

e *Strip 5 at the top is lintel fabric, strip 6 brick fabric.*

f *Strips 7 and 8 are brick fabric.*

Window and door block (B)

To make a front door, make two window blocks beginning as above. Choose a different fabric for the front door, and use this for strip 8 on one of the blocks, as shown, and for strip 7 on the other, so that you have a mirror image. Join the blocks along the door edges to create two windows and a front door.

Roof block (C)

This is assembled in the spiral method.

a *Cut two matching squares, one of roof fabric and one of sky. Cut these diagonally to make two triangles.*

b *Join one triangle of each, and cut the finished piece to the size you want the central square of your block.*

c *Make the left-hand edge of the roof first. Join strip 1 in sky fabric to the sky edge of the central block as shown.*

d *Add strip 2 in roof fabric next down the sky side of the central square as shown. This creates a piece that will look like a chimney, because it's coming up from the roof.*

e *Strips 3 and 4 are roof fabric.*

f *For the final round, strips 5 and 6 are sky, strips 7 and 8 are roof. Make up the second block, for the right-hand side of the roof, as a mirror image.*

A

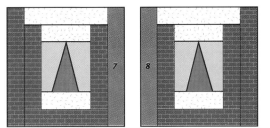

B

C

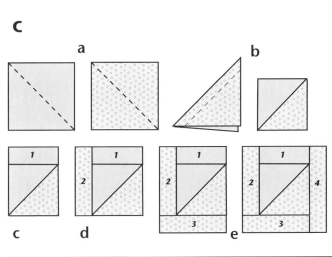

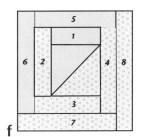

Tree blocks (D)

Make four spiral blocks with strips 1 and 2 in sky fabric, 3 and 4 in foliage, 5 and 6 in sky, and 7 and 8 in foliage. (The foliage could be green for spring or summer, flowered for blossom trees, rust colours for autumn, or even white for a snowy scene.) Join them in a square so that all the foliage sides are together, for a traditional ball-shaped tree (right), or join them so that you have two triangles of foliage to make a pine-tree (below right).

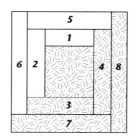

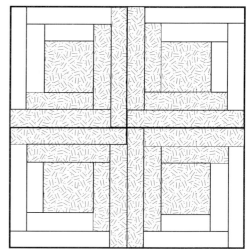

D

Garden blocks (E)

Use either the spiral or the courthouse steps technique to create blocks with various green or floral plain and print fabrics – or use browns and tans if your garden hasn't been planted yet! For a regular effect across the garden, don't divide the block into light and dark.

E
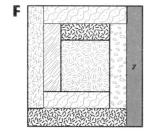

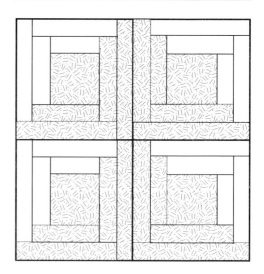

Garden path blocks (F)

Make two spiral blocks using varied floral fabrics, but make strip 8 on one and strip 7 on the other in a different fabric to represent the path. Join the two path sides together to create a small garden that will go underneath a two-block house.

F

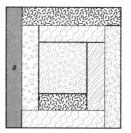

Tree-trunk blocks

Make two garden path blocks as left, but make the contrasting strips brown to create a tree-trunk. Join the two brown sides together to create a tree-trunk in a garden. You can use a trunk like this for a ball-shaped tree, as on the cushion-cover on page 37, or for a fir-tree.

CONTINUOUS PIECING

If you get hooked on log cabin you may want to go into 'mass production' and make several blocks. With continuous piecing you join all the first stages of each block together, then all the second stages etc. Only try this if you're making identical blocks, though, otherwise you'll probably get in a muddle with what goes where.

Sew all the squares to the first strip, leaving a small gap between each square. Trim the strips to size before opening them out; this is very important as the accuracy is maintained by cutting against the previous piece. Iron all the pieces and join the next strip in the same way. This method is particularly useful when the unit is very small as it avoids distortion.

LIBERATED LOG CABIN

This technique is sometimes called crazy log cabin, and that's a good description of it – it's log cabin without having to be accurate!

You cut all the strips by eye instead of using a rotary cutter, then add them round a central shape (this doesn't have to be an accurate square either…) using the spiral method.

FOLDED LOG CABIN

Fine fabrics such as lawn and silk work well in log cabin if you give them extra bulk: one way is by using the folded log cabin technique.

a *Cut the strips of fabric double the normal width and then fold each one in half along its length.*

b *Unfold a strip and position it on your central square as usual, then stitch 1/4in inside the fold.*

c *Press back along the fold again, and continue adding strips in the same way.*

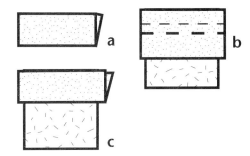

CURVED LOG CABIN

Curved log cabin blocks are constructed using the spiral method: the first two strips added are narrow, then the next two wide, and so on round the block, creating the effect of a curve across the block.

This design can be built into all kinds of secondary patterns, making use of the curve. The drawings below show the effect when the wide strips are in the centre (below left), and when they are on the outside (below right).

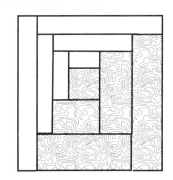

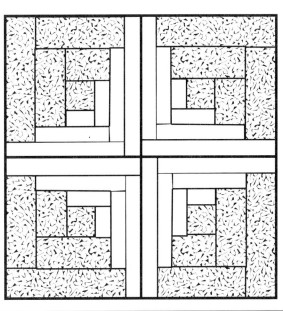

Log Cabin Houses

A while ago I started making 'pictures' in log cabin, and made a house quilt. The Quilt Room in Dorking then asked me to contribute the chapter on log cabin houses in their first book of workshops, and I'm very grateful to them for allowing me to reproduce some of the examples from that book. My life revolves around houses and building. My husband John is a quantity surveyor: in lay terms that means he calculates the costs of each element of a building – fascinating stuff! About 12 years ago he was made redundant from a large architectural firm in London, so we decided to start a business from home.

I was sent on a week's typing course and we converted the children's playroom into an office. This actually was a blessing in disguise; luckily the work came in, and I was stuck to the house. My patchwork productivity went up 100-fold as I didn't go out to coffee or shopping or teaching. I don't feel aggrieved at being tied to the office as the time is never wasted: when I'm not required to type out thrilling plumbing schedules I can get on with my sewing. I was so green at first that answering the phone I made big blunders with builders. When they asked 'Is he in?', I'd reply, 'Sorry, he's tied up at the moment'. The most respectable answer I had to that was 'That sounds painful, darling!'

In 1986 The Quilters Guild had a trip to America – an exchange with quilters in Atlanta and a symposium in North Carolina. I decided to go; this was my first visit to the States. We had to take a quilt for exhibition at the symposium and I made *English Country Garden*. The sky and garden were log cabin, and the thatched cottage was made in blocks with black tape added for the wood framing (see the picture at the top of page 33).

This was much admired, and a lady from Minnesota who had a patchwork shop asked to buy it. I refused at first: I very rarely sell my work, as I feel it's a bit like putting up your children for adoption. I eventually relented, and she then lent it to another quilter in Chesapeake Bay to be exhibited.

This lady then asked me to make a quilt of her own house in the same manner! She sent me a photo, and even requested certain birds and flowers be added. As I hadn't even heard of the flowers and birds, I cheated with Liberty prints. She was very pleased with the result and I subsequently made a few more which were sold in America.

If the idea of making a log cabin picture appeals to you, you could always try interpreting your own house in blocks – see pages 33-34 for basic techniques. Or if you don't fancy doing your own design, try the simple scene on the cushion-cover in the photograph on the right. Instructions for creating this little house and its garden are on pages 38-39.

THE PROJECT

House cushion-cover

These instructions are for a basic house block with garden and one tree; the design would make an ideal housewarming present. It isn't strictly necessary to quilt the cushion cover, but as there are so many small strips in the project it just adds more stability and durability. I find cushions receive more wear than any other patchwork projects, especially with large boys in jeans sitting on them! So it's a good idea not to use very fine lawns for cushions unless they are backed with a stabilising fabric, such as the gridded Vilene.

Choosing the fabrics

It's great fun finding fabrics to represent roofs, walls, flowers, trees and sky. The rule to remember is not to muddle the 'currency': if a certain floral fabric is representing a brick wall it cannot represent a flower bed as this would confuse the eye. I cut up lots of strips with the rotary cutter then bag them up and label them 'sky', 'walls' and so on. The curtains are so small you can use the quilt shop samples – now there's a thrifty idea.

Cutting the fabrics

For the houses I use 1in (2.5cm) strips of fabric, cut with a rotary cutter and a large plastic ruler. This gives a sewn strip of 1/2in (1.2cm); I know this is very small and fiddly, but it gives a lovely result, so either curse me as you piece or enlarge the blocks. The central square for each block is 1 1/2in (3.8cm); this makes it big enough to do the diagonal seam on the roof blocks, and to add the curtains.

✦ MATERIALS

✧ Two 15x9in (38x23cm) rectangles of firm fabric to make the cushion backing
✧ 15in (38cm) square of wadding or dolmette
✧ Scraps of fabric to represent: brick; window lintels (choose a contrast to the brick fabric, possibly a stone effect); curtains (use several different patterns); front door; sky; roof and chimneys; trees; tree trunk; garden; path
✧ Sylko
✧ Anchor quilting thread

✦ METHOD

1 Using the window, curtain, lintel and brick fabrics, make two plain window blocks as described on page 33.

2 Using the same fabrics as above plus the front door fabric, make two mirror-image window-and-door blocks as described on page 33.

3 Cut a two-inch square from the roof fabric and the sky fabric and use these to make the central squares for the roof blocks as shown on page 33. Trim the blocks to 1 1/2in (3.8cm), then use the sky and roof fabrics to build up two mirror-image roof blocks as described.

4 Follow the instructions on page 34 to make two garden-and-path blocks, two tree-trunk blocks, and four tree blocks.

5 Make two more blocks just of sky fabric, using the spiral method.

6 Lay all the blocks out to create a square scene, following the diagram opposite; make sure that you have all the blocks facing in the right direction. Join them in rows, then join the rows together to complete the pattern.

7 Phew! You've now made a house. (It seems a fiddle at first but it's a darn site quicker than real building: as I write I'm in my 13th week of builders in my kitchen...) Now add a 1 1/2in (roughly 4cm) strip of flowered fabric all the way around the scene to give it a frame.

8 Press the scene well from the back and cut a piece of wadding or dolmette to fit the square. Quilt around the house and the tree by hand or machine, then follow the instructions on page 70 to make the square up into a cushion cover.

☞ **TIPS**

If you have the builders in, offer them Earl Grey tea on the first day: they will bring their own in future!

❀

A 6in (15cm) ruler is ideal for making the central squares for the roof blocks as it has a diagonal line to place the pieces on for accuracy.

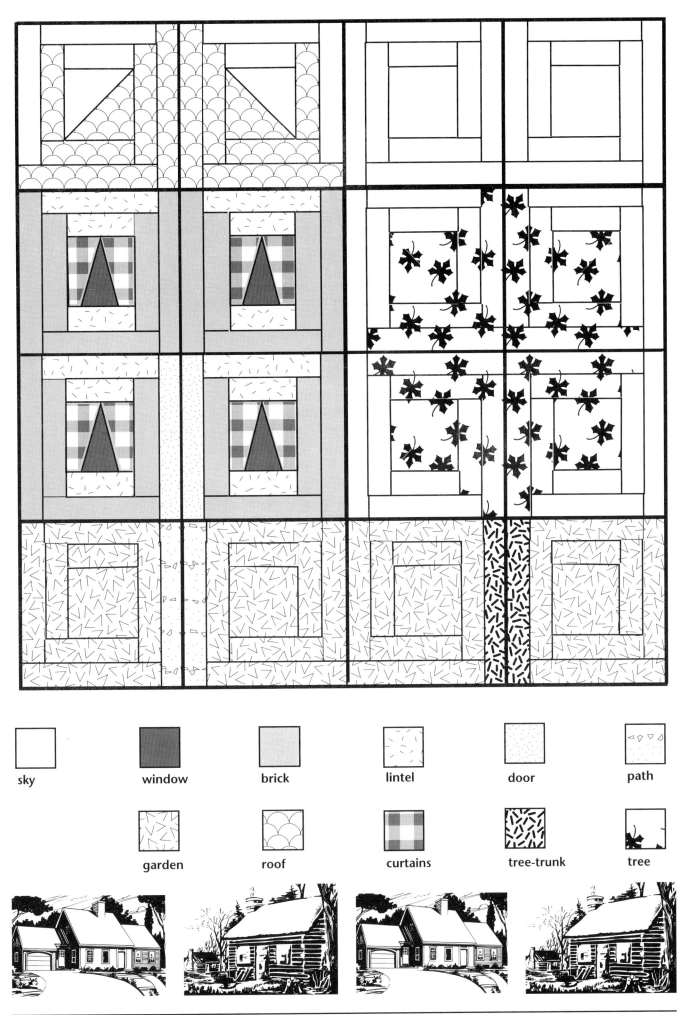

sky   window   brick   lintel   door   path

garden   roof   curtains   tree-trunk   tree

Folded Log Cabin

Folded log cabin is created using the same method as for an ordinary log cabin block (see page 32), but the block is constructed on a foundation backing and each strip is folded before being sewn down. Because each strip is used double, and therefore has more strength than a single layer, it means that you can use flimsy fabrics or other types usually considered unsuitable for log cabin designs. When you're making up folded log cabin you can use either the spiral or the courthouse steps design (see page 32), depending on the effect that you're looking for.

THE PHOTO FRAMES

I had been fiddling about with folded log cabin and realised that because of the method of sewing on the strips, when they were folded back it left a little channel which would hold a photo in place. I then made some for presents and they seemed very popular, as you can make a really personalised present.

I made one for someone who had just redesigned her garden: the frame looked like a pergola or rose arch, with alternate dark and floral strips – it was very effective. I then slipped a photo of her garden into the frame.

I taught my daughter-in-law how to make the frames and she then made some as presents for the baby-clinic girls with their babies' photos. As you can put different-sized photos in, the frames can be used with new photos as a child grows.

THE PROJECT

Log cabin picture frame

☞ TIPS

It's best to iron up some strips first, then arrange them and play around with them till you get a good colour arrangement. This could be complete rounds worked in one colour, changing colour for the next round. Or the whole block could be half light, half dark, like traditional spiral, or you could create a subtle colourwash of the colours across the frame.

❋

Note: a normal photo is 6x4in (15x10cm). If this is critical and you don't want to cut your photo to fit the frame you will have to make the frame 10x8in (25.5x20.5cm).

◆ **MATERIALS**

for an 8in (20cm) frame

✧ 2in (5cm) wide strips of fabric. The longest you will need is 9in (23cm).
✧ A backing fabric of either checked gingham (make sure the squares are accurate) or gridded Vilene 9x9in (23x23cm)
✧ A piece of thick card 8x8in (20x20cm); this can be from a cereal box or similar
✧ 3in (7.5cm) of fine ribbon in a colour to match your frame
✧ Wrapping paper cut 7x7in (18x18cm)
✧ PVA glue, and strong brown parcel tape (optional)

◆ **METHOD**

1 Iron the strips in half so that they are now 1in (2.5cm) wide.

2 On the backing fabric, draw diagonal lines across the square from the corners.

3 Cut a square of fabric 2x2in (5x5cm) and pin it in the centre of the backing fabric; the corners of the squares will fall on the diagonal lines.

4 Position the first strip so that it is on the edge of the central square with the fold towards the centre and the raw edges outwards. Open out the fold and stitch a line of machine stitching just inside the fold (if you run the edge of the machine foot along the fold itself this will work out just right).

5 Fold the strip back to its original size.

6 If you are using the courthouse steps method, as here, add a matching strip the other side of the central square in the same way. If you are using the spiral method, add the second strip down one side and continue working your way around the block.

7 Continue adding strips log-cabin-fashion until the piece measures 7x7in

(18x18cm). Then add an unfolded strip all round; the extra fabric in this strip will be used as the binding of the frame. Iron the patchwork on the back of the work so that the iron won't catch in the folds.

8 Take your square piece of card; lay the patchwork on one side of the card and fold the raw edges around the outside of the card square. Stick them in position on the back of the card with PVA fabric glue – stick opposite sides first to get a tight fit. (You could use brown parcel tape for this if you prefer.)

9 Make a loop of the ribbon, position it in the centre of the frame at the back, and stick it in position.

10 Stick the wrapping paper on the back to cover the raw edges and the loop.

11 Find some nice photos and cut them to fit, hang them on the wall and await the admiring comments.

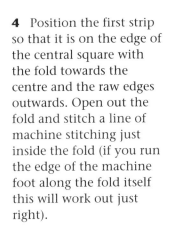

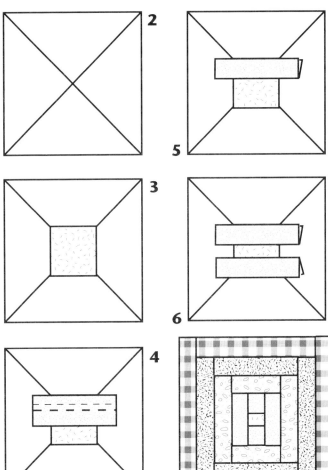

FOLDED LOG CABIN

Curved Log Cabin

This technique is a variation of the basic spiral method of constructing log cabin (see page 32), but by using two different widths for the strips, narrow on one side and wide on the other, it creates the illusion of curves. Curved log cabin can look like a clamshell pattern, and also can be used effectively as hills and sky in landscapes, as I've done in the quilt above and the project inspired by it (opposite). You can piece it by machine as mentioned for the ordinary spiral technique, but I find that this is a good one to do by hand on a foundation backing, as the grid acts as a good stitching guide. I use a Vilene with a grid printed onto it; it only comes in one size – 1cm squares – but you can of course simply use two or three squares at a time if you want larger strips.

THE QUILT

Land of the Long White Cloud

1994
39x38in (99x96.5cm)
NPC

Land of the Long White Cloud is the Maori name for New Zealand. I have a school-friend who lives there, and on one of our visits to Australia to visit our son we returned via New Zealand. The landscape on the quilt is the view from her kitchen window. I embroidered the sheep with lazy daisy stitches and French knots (see page 71); each evening I sat and sewed, and still it seemed to need more sheep.

The borders are to represent the Maori meeting houses. The Maoris paint them this dark red colour, and the houses feature carved symbols of fierce tribesmen who stick their tongues out at visiting dignitaries, and swirling paisley-type patterns which are derived from tree ferns. The shells are paua; I actually bought these in a museum and John painstakingly drilled holes in them so that I could apply them. The other shells are from the beach, and the bone carving is an earring (I lost the other one). So it's a memory quilt of three weeks' holiday.

The quilt is hand-pieced on gridded Vilene as described for the project, and the whole quilt is hand-quilted very

heavily. I marked the patterns with hard soap. When my friend visited me she loved it, so I gave it to her, which is particularly nice as she has now moved to the town. People think I am barmy giving quilts away, but I have an enormous family to give to. I am one of four girls, we have 13 children between us, they have 27 children and we're still counting. So that's a lot of wedding, christening and 21st quilts to make! That's only my side of the family, so I don't have the time or inclination to make quilts to sell.

THE PROJECT
Sheep may safely graze

✦ **MATERIALS**
for a 14¹/2 x18in (37x46cm) hanging
✧ 12 squares of gridded Vilene, each piece 11x11 marked squares
✧ 1in (2.5cm) and 2¹/2in (6cm) strips of fabric in various greens for the hills, some small flowers, and blue for the sky. (The sky is all narrow strips.)
✧ Wide strips of fabric for a striped border, or a suitable border fabric
✧ Wadding, 14¹/2x18in (37x46cm)
✧ Backing fabric, 14¹/2x18in (37x46cm)
✧ Strips of toning fabric to bind the outside of the hanging

✦ **METHOD**
The pieces are put on the front of the fabric (the side without the grid), but are sewn from the back (along the marked grid): this ensures complete accuracy. It seems strange at first as you can't see what you're doing, but it works a treat and your friends will be amazed at your accuracy with small piecing. It's marvellous travel sewing as it can be done by hand and in small units.

1 On each piece of Vilene, count four squares in from the edge and make a mark; do the same on the next side, and draw a square of four blocks on the grid. Make a cross in this with biro. Outside the marked square you should have four grid squares on two sides and five grid squares on the other two sides (see diagram 1 on page 44).

2 Four blocks are skyline: these have the narrow strips as the sky and the wide strips as the hills. Put a wide strip cut into a square on the right side of the Vilene (without the grid) and pin it in position. Put the first narrow strip of sky over it on the side with four squares, and pin it in place.
Instead of sewing this down as normal, turn over to the gridded side and sew along the line over the square

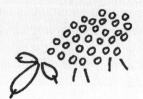

(this covers two squares of the grid). When you have sewn the seam, the right side of the work will look like the diagram.

3 Fold the strip of sky fabric back and press.

4 On the front position the second strip of the sky fabric and sew as previously.

5 Strip 3 is a wide one in a green hill fabric, stitched in the same way.

6 Strip 4 is a second wide green one to complete the round.

7 Continue working round the block in the same way, with strips 5 and 6 in narrow sky fabric, strips 7 and 8 in wide hill fabric. Finish the block with two final strips of narrow sky fabric, as the ninth and tenth strips.

Your block will now look as shown: the dotted line marks the seam allowance. Make up the other three skyline blocks in the same way.

1
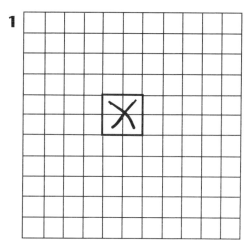

2
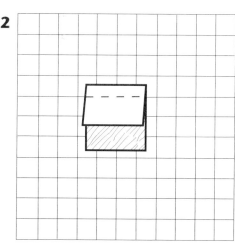

3
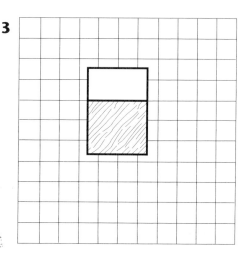

4
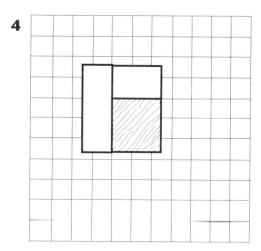

5
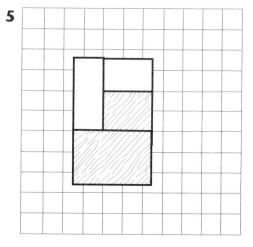

6
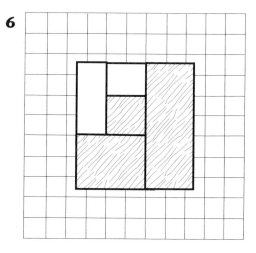

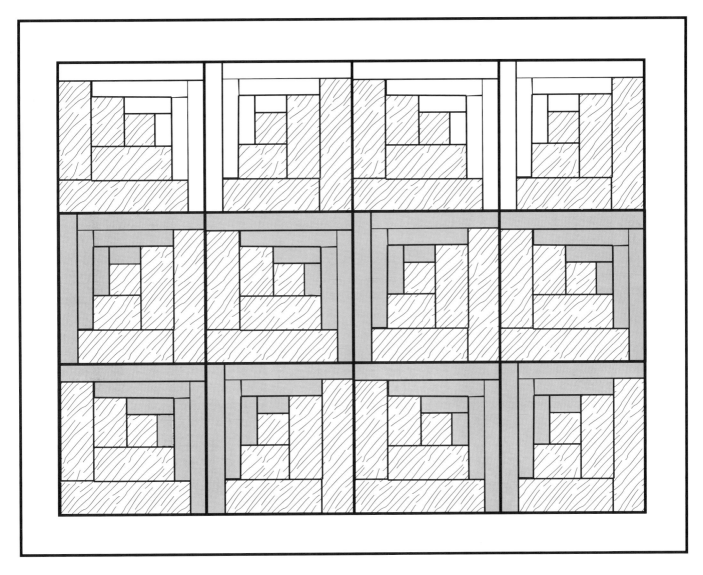

8 Construct the rest of the eight blocks for the panel in the same way, but using various green and floral fabrics to create hills (refer back to the photograph to see how these make hill shapes).

9 Press each block thoroughly and lay them out following the diagram above. Pin the blocks together in rows, then join them by hand; when you place them face to face for sewing the strong lines of the grid are very helpful.

10 Join the rows to complete the patchwork, then add a 2in (5cm) border of plain or patterned fabric in toning colours. I used a border fabric which I mitred at the corners.

11 Make a sandwich with the wadding and backing fabric (see page 70) and pin with safety pins to secure the layers for quilting. Either hand quilt around the hills or free machine quilt as page 17. I used a transparent top thread.

12 Now for the really fun bit! Embroider as many sheep as you want in lazy daisy and French knots (see page 71), following the sheep diagrams opposite.

13 Give it to a friend who visits! Or, if you're sensible, keep it.

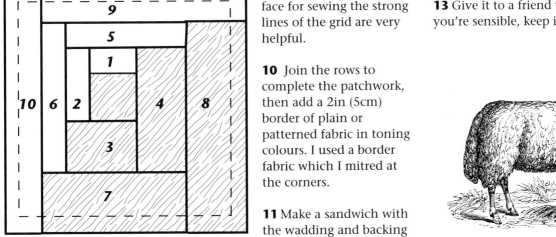

LOG CABIN COMBINATIONS

All the patterns on these two pages are made by combining standard spiral blocks in different ways across your quilt. If you think of a log cabin block as two triangles, you can re-create any design that you can make from combinations of plain squares and triangles. Make a batch of blocks, then try laying them out in different combinations to try out the varied effects.

STREAK O' LIGHTNING

This design of large triangles can be created across a whole quilt design, as here: it also makes a useful edging done in a strip of single blocks – this gives a sawtooth pattern. I've used Streak O' Lightning around a large star-design double quilt, and on my piece Just in Case of Hijack.

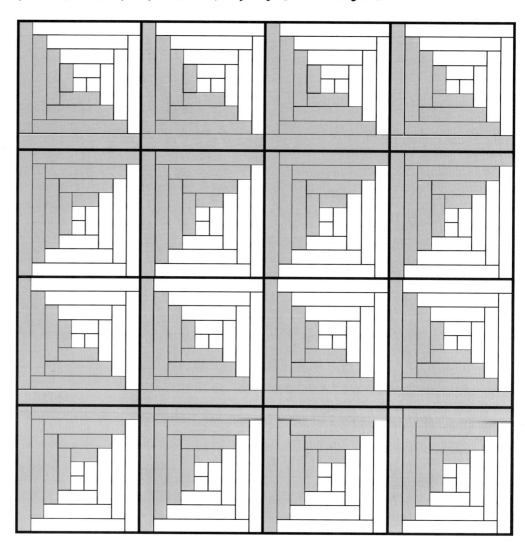

STRAIGHT FURROWS

A very descriptive name for this strong pattern, which as you can see looks like the furrows in a ploughed field.

LOG CABIN STAR

A simple rotation of half the blocks through 180° produces a very effective pattern of triangles. In this design, light edges always join to dark edges: make the quilt up in squares of four blocks, then join the squares.

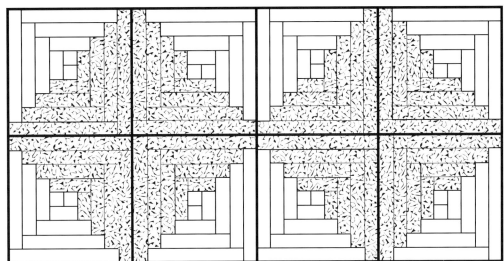

SUNSHINE & SHADOWS

Join four blocks into a square so that their dark sides are towards the centre of the square and the light sides on the outside. As you join the squares, you create an overall pattern of alternating light and dark diamonds.

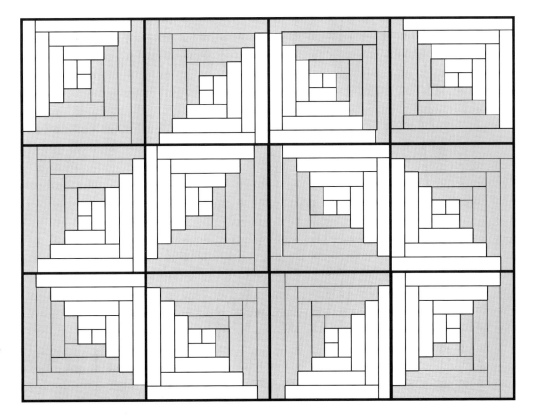

BARN RAISING

This is a larger pattern which creates wide diamond-shaped borders, alternately light and dark, working out from a central diamond. You can continue the pattern outwards as far as you like!
I've used this design for the quilt Blue Lagoon *on page 56; I also used it a while ago for a small hanging in Liberty prints called* Obsession.

Liberated Log Cabin

This technique really combines log cabin and crazy patchwork – a sort of crazy log cabin. Basically you use the same method as for spiral log cabin (page 32), but instead of cutting the strips accurately with a rotary cutter you cut them by eye with scissors, so they come out different widths. The centre square is also cut by eye and therefore is not actually square.

Having strived for years to get my log cabin designs beautifully straight and even, I found it quite difficult to relax into this technique with gay abandon! There's something odd about deliberately cutting fabric inaccurately. Each block is worked on a foundation fabric: this can be any unwanted fabric, or calico, or those old sheets again! I find a 6in (15cm) block works well.

In the photographs opposite you can see two very different developments of the liberated log cabin design. In the main quilt I've used exotic fabrics in blues, golds, creams and black, while the cot quilt below is created in bright children's prints in vivid colours.

THE QUILT
A Night at the Opera

1998
41x45in (104x114cm)
NPC

A Night at the Opera is a departure for me as I've used sparkly fabrics for the first time. I usually use all kinds of outrageous fabrics in my crazy quilts, and lots of tasteful Liberty prints in my log cabin quilts, but this is a first for sparkles and silks. Gail Lawther (who's editing this book) came to talk to the quilt group I belong to and brought little packs of sparkly fabric. I made a few blocks up and rather liked the effect, so mixed the metallic fabric with some silks which a niece had brought back from India.

The title is because the black squares looked like men's dinner jackets and the sparkles the ladies dresses. I kept up the theme by quilting treble clefs with gold thread on the border black ties (made in the bow tie block). As I usually put writing on my quilts I quilted *la, la, la,* and *tra, la, la,* around the edge and on some of the blocks. It was exhibited at the National Patchwork Championships at Olympia in 1998 in The Sky's the Limit category.

THE PROJECT
Ben Bates' quilt

This is a quick and easy cot quilt using lots of childlike prints with the centre 'squares' being bright motifs (on my version they're either teddy prints or cows). The quilt is modelled in the photograph by my granddaughter Alice, but was made for my great nephew Ben who now owns it. I've since added *night night sleep tight mind the bugs don't bite* round the edge, plus his name and birth date to personalise it.

For your quilt look through your fabric bags and pick out brightly-coloured cotton prints as well as any kids' prints featuring strong motifs – teddies, hearts, cars, ladybirds, rainbows, butterflies, whatever. These are great for the centrepieces.

I was able to make Ben's quilt entirely out of scrap fabric and offcuts, but if you don't think you've got enough suitable scraps buy a bit of bright striped or checked fabric to pad it all out – designs like that are often cheaper than the more specialised prints. You can use plain fabrics in vivid colours, too, of course.

◆ **MATERIALS**
  for a 24-block quilt 26x38in (66x96.5cm)
◇ 2½in (6cm) wide strips of border fabric (I used clouds, but you could use any suitable print or plain fabric): two strips 26in(66cm) long, and two strips 38in (96.5cm) long
◇ Calico or waste fabric for 24 6in (15cm) blocks

LIBERATED LOG CABIN

- ✧ Various strips of different brightly-coloured children's fabrics, roughly cut into strips varying from 1½in (3cm) to 2in (5cm) wide
- ✧ Bright backing fabric 28x40in (71x102cm). This will be brought round from the back to the front to form a binding.
- ✧ 2oz wadding, 26x38in (66x96.5cm)

✦ METHOD

1 Cut 24 6in (15cm) squares of calico or waste fabric. Choose motifs (eg teddies, cars, hearts) that will be suitable for the block centres and cut them out in rough squares. Put one of the motifs in the middle of one of the pieces of calico and position the first rough-cut strip face-down at the top, just as you would for making a spiral log cabin block.

2 Machine-stitch the first strip down onto the foundation, then flip it over and press it well.

3 Choose a strip in a colour and design that contrasts well with the centre patch and the first strip, and add it down the side of the block in the same way.

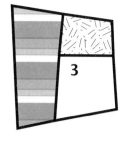

4 Add the third strip along the bottom of the centre motif.

5 Add a fourth strip down the right-hand side to complete the first round of the block.

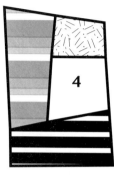

6 Continue adding strips around the block in a spiral until you have covered the foundation fabric thoroughly. You will probably get three rounds of the strips on a foundation block of this size, depending on the width of the strips used.

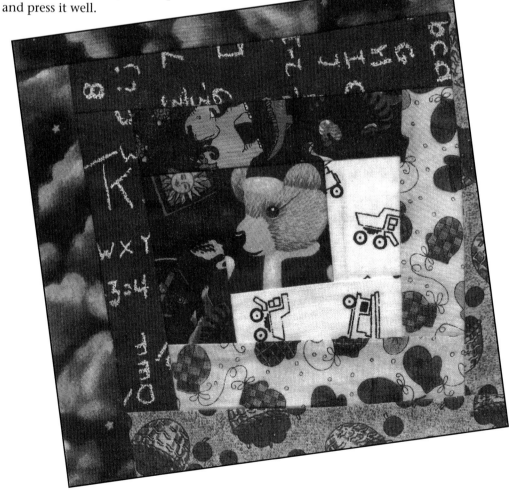

7 When all 24 blocks are completed iron them thoroughly. Check each block for size and trim it back to 6in (15cm) square if necessary.

8 Arrange the blocks in a rectangle four across and six down (sounds like a crossword clue!) Take your time to find the best arrangement: some colours might be more dominant than others, so try looking at the layout with a door spy (see page 10).

9 Machine the blocks together in rows, then open the seams out flat on the back and press them open so that they lie as flat as possible – the added bulk of the extra fabric makes it impractical to press the seams to one side. Now stitch the rows together to complete the patchwork.

10 Add the border strips round the edges of the assembled blocks by machine, then press thoroughly.

11 Lay the backing fabric right side down on a flat surface and position the wadding on top: lay the patchwork right side up on top of the wadding so that there is an even border of backing fabric all round the edges. Turn this extra fabric over to the front of the quilt in a double fold and hem it down to make the binding.

12 Embroider the child's name and date of birth, and don't forget to sign your own name.

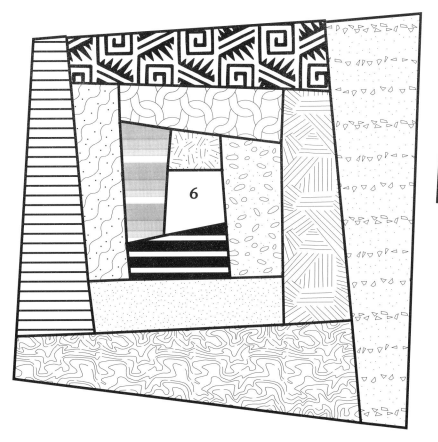

☞ **TIP**
Keep a record book of your work, with photos and actual pieces of the fabrics. This can be in plastic pockets in a loose-leaf folder. It's a nice memory, especially if, like me, you give a lot of the finished quilts away.

CHAPTER 3

FUN WITH FABRIC

*T*his section is a pot-pourri of various unusual techniques which I have found make unique effects for quilts. Don't feel you have to stick to traditional methods for creating your quilts: all the best patterns and techniques were new once – we draw on the creativity and individuality of millions of quilters who have gone before us. Why not add your individual mark to quilting in the 21st century by experimenting with unusual techniques?

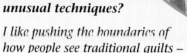

I like pushing the boundaries of how people see traditional quilts – developing traditional techniques, as in the previous sections, and trying out new ones, as in this section. These days there are so many more things available to the quilter that our forebears would have given their eye teeth for – metallic fabrics and threads, exotic silks and satins, rainbow threads, unusual machine stitches (and sewing machines themselves…), easy-to-use dyes and fabric paints, plus an endless supply of beads and other embellishments from around the world.

In this section I particularly concentrate on ways in which you can enhance, embellish or manipulate the fabrics you are using for your quilts. Do try these techniques, as they can make your quilt something very different from everyone else's, and truly your own work.

Machine quilting

Using machine quilting for 'drawing' with your needle can create a really individual effect that you can suit to the quilt in hand. Who has decreed that filler patterns should always be vermicelli? I prefer different kinds of pasta. In this section you'll find some designs and ideas from my quilts; try them out, or develop your own.

Using bleach

Tie-dye effects can be produced in reverse by using bleach: some cheap dark fabric can be transformed into fantastic patterns and colours in seconds. You can then use the patterned fabrics you've created to add a new twist to traditional piecing, as in this dramatic 'gentleman's comforter'.

Black on black

This is an appliqué method which looks very intricate but is in fact a big cheat! In this section you'll learn how to make the most of fabrics with dark backgrounds and use them to create your own spectacular designs.

Hammered leaves and flowers

Old sheets can be made into works of art with only a little hammer power; hammering leaves and flowers releases the pigments from their fibres and produces a delicately beautiful – and permanent – effect that's very realistic. Be warned, though: if you're reading this in the winter you'll have to be patient and wait until spring for the flowers and leaves to appear.

MACHINE QUILTING

As I mentioned on page 17, when I was experimenting with machine quilting I discovered that by dropping the feed dogs I could 'draw' freehand patterns with the stitching. My first attempt was on my quilt *The Red Wine Equation* (see photo below). This was a quilt trying to look like a school maths book. The government had issued an edict that red wine was now considered positively good for your health; this was good news for me as I have an allergy to white wine.

I used pictograms to create simple equations in the centre, like:

then I scribbled with my needle all round the borders, drawing wine-related things: bottles, glasses, corkscrews, vine leaves and bunches of grapes.

I then added typical teachers' remarks: 'Please stop scribbling in the margin: see me'. Freehand writing with your machine is a jolly good way of practising free machining: try writing your name first – and aren't you the lucky one if it's something like Ann rather than Dorothy with a t to cross. To begin with this technique seems impossible, but persevere: you'll suddenly get the hang of it, and it's well worth persisting.

One quilt in which the entire background is machine-embroidered writing is *I'm Only A Mum* (see the quilt on the wall on page 20). It depicts a Mum wearing all the hats one needs: a mortar board, a nurse's hat, a sports hat, a woolly hat and a halo. She is juggling balls with all the impossible questions children ask embroidered on them, such as:

- Why isn't tea ready
- Why do birds have white poos
- What is 9468 X 3¹/₄
- What does **** mean
- Who is God's Daddy

The background writing was in black thread on green fabric and was continuous Mummy Mum Mom Ma Mother. The Mother was a pain, having to go back and cross the T's after I'd finished the word.

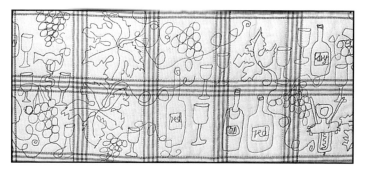

In my quilt *Blue Lagoon* (see page 56) the quilting is fish, drawn freehand using variegated machine thread. This is useful stuff; it comes in many different colour schemes and so gives a subtle random colour change and a pleasant effect. I foolishly decided to give the fish eyes, which meant hundreds of hand-sewn french knots.

In *Take Time to Smell The Flowers* (see page 64) I used a flower motif. I stitched it in transparent thread, but it would have been just as effective with white thread. If I doodle on a telephone pad I tend to draw little flowers.

The drawings and photographs on these pages show you just some of the many ways you can use free machine quilting to draw designs: try a few out on your machine, then develop your own ones. Don't try and copy the designs here exactly: the whole essence of free quilting is a nice loose, free movement and pleasing, flowing lines.

Using Bleach

Making discharged patterns with bleach is really tie-dye in reverse: the fabric is bound and tied, and when it's immersed in bleach the dye is released from the exposed areas. This can create some fascinating colours and textures, and you can build the finished results into your work, as I've done with the large and small quilts opposite. Bleaching is always an experiment, as some fabrics discharge brilliantly and others don't. The plus side is that if you do this technique in the kitchen sink the bleach cleans both the sink and the drains at the same time! Who could ask for more?

I use ordinary household bleach, and I find the thick sort works best. Of course if it bleaches the fabric it will also bleach your clothes, so this is an old-clothes, rubber-gloves, window-open technique. If you're a very messy worker and feel you might splash bleach too far, do it in the garden (covering your table with plastic sheeting) and have a bucket of rinsing water ready.

Initially I found that the trouble with discharging is making it stop. Hydrogen peroxide works best: you can get it from pharmacies, and it stops the discharge reaction. I've also heard that Campden tablets, used for sterilising wine- and beer-making equipment, work in the same way. The fibres of the fabric will be weakened if the bleach is left on for too long, so it's important to find fabrics which will discharge easily and quickly. This, I'm afraid, is 'try it and see'.

THE QUILT

Blue Lagoon

1998
45x51in (114x129.5cm)
EQC

I made this quilt in the summer of 1997. My great friend, the embroiderer Linda Tudor, and I were having a dyeing day in the garden. I as usual was in a right old mess, so had the bleach out to try and clean up a bit. I found that some Nancy Crowe fabric in blue stripes discharged into incredible colours, ranging from turquoise to pink. I only had half a metre of the fabric so I cut it into strips and discharged the lot.

I was so excited at the result that I thought I would buy some more of the fabric – of course not available any more, so I had to be inventive with what I had. I made it in log cabin and it began to look like a Caribbean reef. As I had limited fabric I cut up a block to make the triangular sides, and the last little scraps are the prairie points. I then free-quilted the whole lot with fish shapes (see page 55) in variegated blue thread.

A few Christmases ago we were lucky enough to be invited by some friends to sail in a small yacht off the Grenadine islands in the Caribbean. We visited a reef in the small tender boat and everyone snorkelled (except me!) I'm terrified of water: I only learnt to swim when I was over 40. I was shamed into it by meeting a lady at a party who likened something to riding a bike:

when I said I couldn't ride a bike she was horrified, and doubly so when I boasted that I also couldn't swim.

The children's primary school had adult swimming lessons so I joined them: it was incredible to hear huge hunky men admitting that they were terrified of water – one even hated having his hair washed. We all learnt successfully, and now I'm even brave enough to swim in deep sea, but snorkelling and meeting fish face to face was a different matter. So I stayed in the small boat and looked over the edge, into wonderful colours of water peopled by small blue fish with bright eyes. I've tried to convey this idea in the quilt.

By the way, I subsequently learnt to ride a bike. John bought me one for my 50th birthday, not really believing that I couldn't ride it. He took me to a station car park on a Saturday when no one was around, and held the back as you do with 6-year-olds – so embarrassing. I suddenly got the hang of it, but was so excited I forgot to steer and hit a bollard. I was a wow at the black-tie dinner in my honour that night with sticking plaster on my knees and elbows. I'm afraid to say the bike is still in the garage unused.

THE PROJECT
Gentleman's Comforter

This is a lap quilt. In the old days they used to be called gentlemen's comforters, which is rather a lovely name. I've used black fabric which was bleached by wrapping it as for tie-dye (see opposite); this came out black, white and a fawn colour in the most surprising patterns. You could use any other plain-coloured fabric, but test a bit in the bleach first to make sure it gives a good discharge. The patchwork pieces are large and simple in order to show off the bleached areas to good advantage. The finished quilt is tied with bright stranded cotton, but if you prefer it could also be hand or machine quilted.

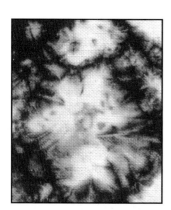

✦ MATERIALS
for a 36x52in (92x132cm) quilt
- ✦ 35 black 6in (15.5cm) squares
- ✦ Enough bleached fabric for at least 35 6in (15.5cm) squares
- ✦ Strips of black fabric 40x4in (101x10cm) and 56x4in (142x10cm) for binding
- ✦ Polyester 2oz or similar wadding 36x52in (92x132cm)
- ✦ Red or bright-coloured backing fabric 36x52in (92x132cm) – for extra comfort use a Viyella or warm brushed cotton fabric
- ✦ Black Sylko
- ✦ Red Anchor stranded cotton for tying
- ✦ Safety pins for 'tacking' the layers together.
- ✦ 6in (15.5cm) square ruler or 6in (15.5cm) template made from stiff see-through plastic. This can be positioned over your discharged fabric so that you can see where the most interesting bits of the pattern are.

✦ METHOD
1 Use a rotary cutter and the template to cut 35 interesting squares from the bleached fabric. Cut all the squares, plain and bleached, diagonally across the middle to make triangles.

2 Machine the triangles into pairs, one plain and one bleached, along the longest side; this can be done in a production-line method. Open all the seams and press them well.

3 Lay the squares out in a pattern of 7 x 10 blocks, keeping all the bleached triangles in the same direction (see photograph on page 56). Move the blocks around until you have a pleasing distribution of the bleached designs.

4 Pin and sew the blocks together in rows of seven, then press the work thoroughly.

5 Pin and sew the rows together to complete the quilt top.

6 Lay the backing fabric right side down on a flat surface and cover it with the wadding, smoothing out the layers thoroughly. Lay the patchwork on top of the wadding, right side up, then pin with safety pins at close intervals.

7 Bind the edges of the quilt with the long strips of black fabric.

8 At each junction between squares, on the quilt front, tie a reef knot in red thread (remember these from Guides?) Thread a needle, take a small stitch at the junction, then tie left over right followed by right over left. Cut off the thread.

9 Sit the gentleman down in his favourite chair, give him a drink and the newspaper and cover him with his comforter. It's a wonderful way of saving on the central heating bill!

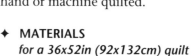

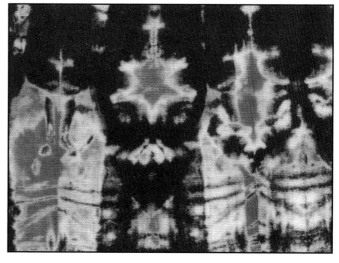

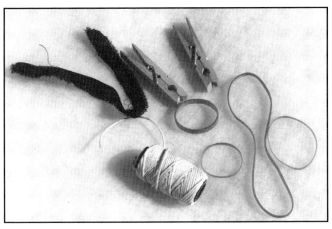
Various items can be used to create patterns

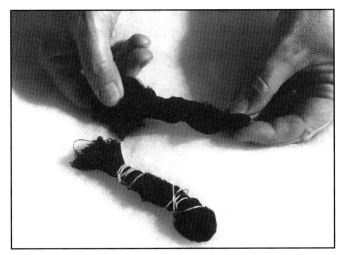
Folded strips of fabric tied in bundles

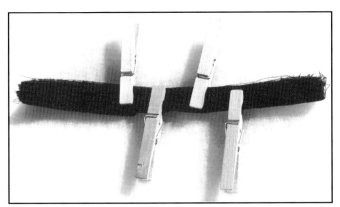
Folded strips pegged at intervals

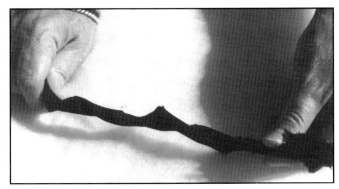
Folded strip twisted and knotted

Bleaching
Basic procedure

1 *Prepare a stop-bath of 10 parts water to 1 part hydrogen peroxide in a plastic bucket or large bowl (remember: don't mix your cooking bowls with bowls for dyeing and discharging).*

2 *If you're not in the garden, open the windows to avoid fumes, and cover your working surface with newspapers or plastic sheeting or both. Wear rubber gloves, and old clothes or a plastic apron (sounds like the operating theatre…)*

3 *Prepare your fabric pieces by knotting them, or tying them up in different ways as shown in the photographs; then immerse each piece in a jamjar or small dish of bleach. Alternatively, you can drop the bleach onto the fabric with a medicine dropper (the sort used for eye drops), or dab it on with cotton buds.*

4 *Turn the sample around in the bleach to get an even distribution, and when the colour begins to lift and be released into the water, take the fabric out.*

5 *Submerge the sample in the stop-bath for five minutes (it fizzes slightly, so don't be alarmed), then wash it well in soapy water.*

6 *Unpick or cut the ties very carefully. Ooh and aah at the amazing results, wash again and dry ready for use.*

TIE DYE

You can use various things to tie up the fabric to get a good resist and create great patterns:

- *String and twine: try different thicknesses*
- *Pegs, wooden and plastic*
- *Rubber bands of different thicknesses*
- *Small stones with rubber bands around them*
- *Dried peas likewise*
- *Strips of fabric (discarded selvedge strips are ideal)*
- *Paper clips*
- *Pipecleaners*
- *Sticks or plastic pipes to wrap fabric around*

Black on Black

A real cheat, this: it's a very quick and easy way of producing what looks like a very intricate and time-consuming appliqué design. The secret lies in the choice of fabrics: all the applied flowered pieces are cut from fabrics with black backgrounds. The shapes are cut out roughly, then stitched to a plain black background fabric – so all the flowers look as though they've been painstakingly appliquéd individually!

The method is a variation of the technique called broderie persé. Broderie persé is a method of appliqué dating from the early 19th century, when chintz fabrics were very expensive to import into Britain from the East and so had to be used sparingly. A large quilt or cushion cover could be made from a small piece of chintz by cutting out the individual flowers and motifs and then applying them onto a background fabric with blanket stitch.

There are various ways of doing this black on black technique: choose the one that suits you best. You can fuse the pieces in position with Bondaweb, or simply tack them in place then appliqué them by hand or machine. You can also use the freezer paper method as described on page 72. If you want to stitch the patches on by hand, you can slipstitch them, or follow the style of the original broderie persé workers and embellish them with blanket stitch (see page 71).

If you have a problem finding suitable fabrics keep an eye out at charity shops; dresses in flowered patterns on black backgrounds were very fashionable a few years ago. In any case charity shops and jumble sales can be Aladdin's caves of wonderful patchwork materials – why not recycle old clothes into works of art? This is a technique which is good to do in a group so that there are lots of 'swaps'. There's no reason why you can't use another colour for all the backgrounds, but black seems to work the best – it's amazing how many variations there can be of other colours, even cream!

THE QUILT
The Sailor's Return

1988
36x30ins (92x76cm)
*Fire and Iron Gallery,
Leatherhead*

I made this quilt many years ago after learning the technique with some sewing friends. Pilgrim Quilters, the quilt group I belong to, were having a Valentine's exhibition so I made it to fit the theme.

I based the design on a Picasso drawing of two hands holding a bunch of flowers, which I'd had on a birthday card from some friends some time previously. On the Picasso print, one hand holds out a bunch of brightly-coloured flowers while the other hand reaches out to receive it.

On my quilt, the flowers are produced with the broderie persé pieces on a black background. One of the hands belongs to the sailor, as I wanted to incorporate the visual patterns of the tattoos; these were inspired by a man in my local post office at the time who had HATE tattooed on the fingers of one hand and LOVE on the other... I drew the tattoos with soft pencil then quilted them in a contrasting cotton thread.

I produced the whole design by hand, with hand appliqué and quilted flower shapes in black; to help me get good shapes for the hands I used the freezer paper technique (see page 72). This

method is a great way of working with difficult shapes, as it holds the turnings in place well while you stitch and creates a firm edge which looks impressive.

Choose fabrics with strong, colourful designs on a solid black background: any of the ones shown here would work well for the technique. Pick small prints for the basket – as you can see from the photograph above, you can either weave two different prints or make the whole basket from one fabric.

THE PROJECT
Flower-basket cushion

This is a rather jolly, bright cushion that can easily be made in an afternoon – and, being black, it's practical too as it won't show the dirt... The flower theme would make it particularly nice for a conservatory or for a garden chair. The bouquet is made from the flower prints, and the basket is woven from two toning fabrics printed with tiny patterns.

✦ MATERIALS
for a 14in (35cm) cushion:
- ✧ 15in (38cm) square of black fabric
- ✧ 15in (38cm) square of 2oz wadding
- ✧ 15x17in (38x43cm) piece of black fabric for the back of the cushion
- ✧ 2yd (2m) of piping cord
- ✧ 10in (25.5cm) black zip fastener
- ✧ 2yd (2m) strip of flowered fabric for the piping, 1in (2.5cm) wide
- ✧ Roughly 4in (10cm) square scraps of 10–12 different flowered fabrics with black backgrounds
- ✧ 8x5in (20x13cm) cream fabric with small printed pattern
- ✧ 8x5in (20x13cm) brown fabric with small printed pattern
- ✧ Small amount of Bondaweb
- ✧ Tracing paper and pencil for the pattern
- ✧ Black Sylko
- ✧ Black Anchor quilting thread
- ✧ 14in (35cm) square cushion pad

> ☞ **TIP**
> Use a cushion pad one size larger than your cover: this makes a lovely plump cushion.

✦ METHOD
1 Cutting in smooth curves around the flower shapes, cut 10 or 12 roughly circular shapes about 3in (7-8cm) in diameter. If you have single blooms that are quite large, follow the shape of the flower more closely, but remember to leave some black at the edges. Iron a 1in (2.5cm) square of Bondaweb to the centre back of each patch; these little pieces will just help to keep the patches in position while you arrange and stitch them.

2 Trace the basket pattern on page 63 onto the tracing paper and cut it out. Cut two 8x5in (cm) pieces of Bondaweb, and iron one onto the back of the cream fabric and one onto the back of the brown fabric. Use a rotary cutter to cut the pieces into 1/2in (1cm) strips, or mark the strips with pencil and cut them out with scissors.

3 Using the tracing paper pattern as a guide, cut the horizontal cream strips to length, cutting the ends at a slant as on the tracing. Remove the backing paper and position the strips on the black background square, with the base section about 2in (5cm) up from the bottom edge of the square and equidistant from the edges. Carefully iron just the edge at one side of each strip to anchor it while you weave the basket.

4 Cut the vertical brown strips to length in the same way and weave them through the cream strips (see diagram). When you are happy with the woven pattern, iron the shapes to fuse them to the background – use a steam iron, or spray the design with water before ironing.

5 Now for the flower arranging! Arrange the flowered patches above the basket to create a pleasing design; some can droop down over the edge of the basket, or may even have dropped to the floor. Take some care over this, and stand back from the arrangement occasionally so that you can get a good look at it. If you have one, use your door spy as described on page 10; this will give you a sense of how the overall design of your flower-basket is working.

When you're happy with the arrangement, iron the shapes as before to fuse them in position. As you've only used a small amount of Bondaweb underneath the edges will still be loose, so you might want to pin or tack them too for extra security as you stitch.

6 Pin the decorated square, right side up, to the wadding, and use black thread and your chosen method of appliqué to attach the patches. You can do this in

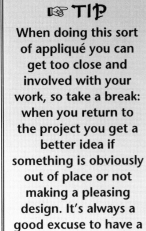

☞ TIP

When doing this sort of appliqué you can get too close and involved with your work, so take a break: when you return to the project you get a better idea if something is obviously out of place or not making a pleasing design. It's always a good excuse to have a cuppa!

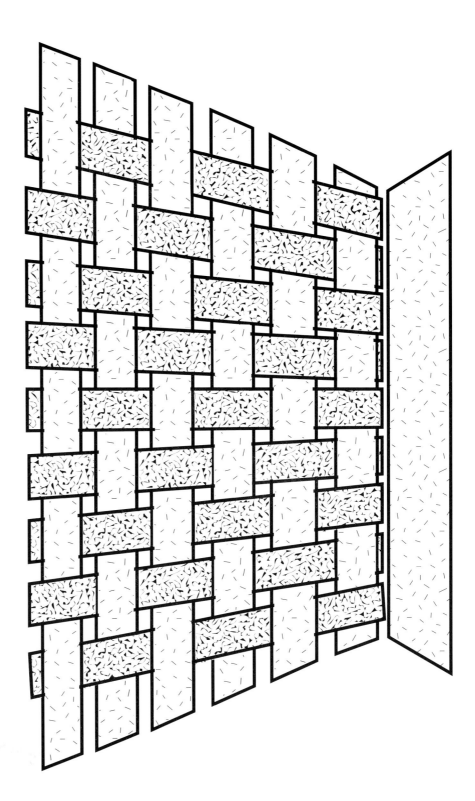

various ways, depending on the effect you want to achieve:

- appliqué by hand with a small hemming stitch
- appliqué by machine with zigzag or a fancy machine stitch – for instance, my machine has a stitch which if used in reverse looks just like blanket stitch. Try out your machine's different stitches on a piece of scrap fabric: you may discover one or two that give a lovely decorative effect.

- broderie persé style with hand-worked blanket stitch in black sewing thread or one strand of black stranded cotton. Blanket stitch is a particularly good one for this technique, as it slightly seals the raw edges of the fabric within the stitching line and stops them from fraying.

7 Make up the cushion cover as described on page 71, then open the zip and insert the cushion pad.

Hammered leaves and flowers

This is a rather hit and miss technique (no pun intended). I first saw this technique described in *The American Quilter* magazine and couldn't wait for the summer to try it out. I then became obsessed with it, commandeering my husband's hammer, getting muscles in my upper arms, and eventually producing my quilt *Take Time To Smell the Flowers*, shown in the large photograph opposite.

What you're doing in this technique is transferring the natural dyes found in plants and leaves onto fabric: the pressure of the hammering makes the dyes migrate from the plantstuff into the fibres of the material. First of all the receiving fabric has to be mordanted: this involves soaking it in a chemical mixture to give it a 'tooth' which makes it receptive to the dye (*mordre* is the French word for bite).

Some plants and flowers work very well and some not, so I'm afraid it's a case of experimenting and making notes for future reference. The time of year also seems to make a huge difference: I used nettles in the late summer, and the resulting print was browner than the ones hammered in May. As you can't always guarantee the exact results I find it better to hammer a selection of leaves, then cut out the best ones and appliqué them to a background fabric. I've designed a mirror frame using nettle leaves as an easy project for trying out this technique, as nettles tend to give a consistently good result.

THE QUILT
Take Time to Smell the Flowers

1997
50x62in (127x157.5cm)
NPC
EQC

The embroiderer Constance Howard had admired my quilt *The Sailor's Return* (page 61) at an exhibition, and said I should pursue the bunch of flowers idea. Having spent the summer trying out the hammering technique, annoying the family with the constant noise and being stared at by passers-by as I plucked nettles, I decided to develop the flower theme using some of my trial pieces.

I had amassed a bag full of prints – some lovely, but some just a blurred mess. I selected the best ones and ironed Bondaweb on the back of them, then cut them out in smooth curves leaving a generous edge: this negates the problem of cutting round all the fiddly serrated edges of the leaves. I then arranged them on a white fabric background, which has a self-coloured flower pattern on it like a damask tablecloth.

When I was happy with the arrangement I ironed the flower and leaf prints to bond them to the background, adding the stalks with grass prints. (These actually faded, which was rather annoying when you think how grass stains when you sit on it in white shorts... The problem was resolved by drawing the lines in brown Pigma pen.)

I machine-quilted the whole piece with transparent quilting thread, free quilting in flower shapes (see the design on page 55). It was the first time I had tried this sort of quilting, and initially I found that it made my neck ache with concentrating; I overcame this by making the machine go half speed and keeping the foot hard down, which made the task much easier.

I added the embroidered label with *Take Time to Smell the Flowers*. The border is vine leaves, nettles and sage. When it was exhibited no one knew it was mine, as it was so tasteful and done in such refined colours!

THE PROJECT
Nettle mirror frame

This frame could be adapted to any size depending what size mirror you can get hold of. I'd intended to use a mirror tile but they seem to be getting scarce, so I went to my local glass shop and they cut me an offcut very cheaply.

The card frame could be cut to size from old boxes or mounting card, but I found it quicker and easier to buy a ready-cut card mount from my local photographic shop. This would also be a good way of using up those mounts from school photographs – probably like me you have a drawerful collected over the years! The card on them is a bit thin so might need backing with a further sheet of card, possibly old cereal boxes (we are definitely into recycling here).

✦ **MATERIALS**
for a 10x12in (25.5x30.5cm) mirror, finished size

✧ Thick card mount 10x12in (25.5x30.5cm) with a 2¼in (5.5cm) border
✧ Offcuts of wadding to fit the frame
✧ White fabric (this could have a patterned weave) 12x14in (30.5x35.5cm)
✧ Hammered nettles (see pages 67-68)
✧ Bondaweb
✧ White Sylko
✧ Spray adhesive or PVA glue
✧ Mirror cut to 9x10in (23x25.5cm)
✧ Brown parcel tape
✧ Sticky tape or masking tape
✧ 27in (70cm) thin white piping cord (optional)
✧ Stick-on strong disc plate-hanger and self-adhesive tabs (from DIY shops)
✧ Thick card 9¾x11¾in (25x30cm)
✧ Sheet of flowered wrapping paper

✦ **METHOD**

1 Cut the wadding to fit over the card mount and stick it in position either with spray glue or PVA.

2 Lay the white fabric right side down and place the card mount over it so that there is an even border all round. Draw round the centre area with pencil. Cut out the middle section of fabric, leaving a 2in (5cm) border inside the drawn line. Now carefully make a diagonal cut into each corner of the drawn pencil line.

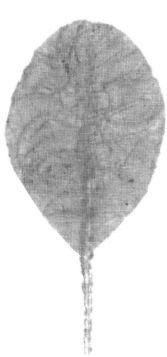

HAMMERED LEAVES AND FLOWERS

3 Turn back all sides of the fabric and stick the shape to the card mount with a few pieces of sticky tape. (This is a temporary measure so that you can put the leaves in the correct place on the frame.)

4 Iron Bondaweb onto the back of the printed nettles and cut out each one, leaving a generous edge. Arrange these shapes around the frame till you get a pleasing design – you could add other flowers or leaves at this stage if you like.

5 Peel off the paper back of the Bondaweb and fuse the shapes down onto the frame. Remove the sticky tape and press the fabric to make the leaves adhere really strongly. There is always a slightly herby smell from the leaves when you press them!

6 Sew the leaves in place with a close zigzag or a fancy machine stitch. Alternatively they can be buttonhole stitched (see page 71) with a white thread.

7 Stick the fabric to the mount either with strong brown parcel tape or PVA glue. Do the top and bottom first, then the sides, to get a nice tight fit over the mount and wadding. Then stick the inner edges down to the back of the mount in the same way.

8 Cut the wrapping paper 1in (2.5cm) larger all round than the thick card. Stick it over one side of the card, mitring the corners. On the side which is not covered by wrapping paper, draw diagonal lines from corner to corner in each direction. These act as guides for placing the mirror: fix it in place with the self-adhesive tabs, so that each corner is on one of the diagonal lines.

9 Try the frame out on the mirror piece. You will find that the mirror reflects the back slightly at the edges, particularly on the corners. To avoid this, either stick a strip of white fabric across each corner on the back of the frame section, or add a border of white piping cord round the inner edge of the frame.

10 Cover the border of card outside the mirror generously with PVA glue, and position the frame section on top. Place the whole mirror face down under a pile of books for a few hours to get a really good adhesion. Those quilting books do have other uses!

11 Stick a disc plate hanger on the back. Hang in a prominent place, and look back at your smiling face.

The Hammering Technique

PREPARING THE FABRIC

Any well-washed 100% cotton fabric will do. It has to be fine enough to make a good print, but strong enough to withstand the hammering, and to pick up the subtle colours it's best to use white, cream or a very pale colour. I used the stronger outer bits of old sheets (something else to look out for at jumble sales!)

For a yard/metre of cloth put a pint of hot water in a plastic bucket and dissolve 2oz (50g) of alum in it. You can buy alum at most pharmacies; it's used in natural wool dyeing, and I am told was an old recipe for curing mouth ulcers! Therefore I presume that it's non-poisonous, but I think a sensible safeguard with any dyeing is not to use kitchen utensils which are also used for food preparation. As I don't have another set of weighing scales I put the alum in a plastic bag so it isn't in direct contact with the scales.

After the mixture has cooled, add a teaspoonful of washing soda crystals (you can buy these from supermarkets) which have been dissolved in hot water. When you add the soda the mixture will bubble up, so don't be alarmed.

Add enough cold water to make the mixture up to a gallon, and soak the fabric for eight hours or overnight. Discard the alum solution and dry the fabric naturally.

CHOOSING LEAVES

As I said, this is a hit and miss technique, so experiment. My findings are that most weeds work well, particularly nettles (what a creative way of weeding the garden this could be). Edible plants often work well: parsley, thyme, vine leaves, fennel, marjoram. Grey-leafed varieties such as Artemesia give good results; they actually print as green. Tree leaves that I've made effective prints with are young horse chestnut, elderberry, dogwood and beech (including copper beech). Dark-purple-leaved plants come out a rather dark blue colour.

CHOOSING FLOWERS

Flowers aren't as consistently successful as leaves. Some varieties which initially looked fantastic, such as lilies, geraniums, lobelia and some bright red flowers, faded to nothing when fixed. I have had considerable success with the daisy family: yellow Rudbeckia are particularly good. Alchemilia Molis (Lady's Mantle) is a good choice: both the flowers and the leaves come out a nice mustard colour. A purple Cosmos came out an acid green. So be warned: the final colour bears no resemblance to the original plant!

The strongest dye is in the stamens, so you might need to remove some with tweezers before hammering so that their dye doesn't blur the rest of the print. Very bulky flowers are more successful if you remove the petals first; then tape these back in position with just a few stamens in the centre. Grasses work well, particularly the frondy sorts, and the seeds come out orange.

HAMMERING

Pick the leaf or flower and immediately prepare it for hammering.

a Place the leaf onto the mordanted fabric, with the vein side towards the cloth.

b Stick it down with strips of masking tape. Either use enough tape around the edges to hold it in place or, with bulky flowers, try and cover the whole flower with the tape. Turn the fabric over so that the taped leaf is on the underside, then lay the fabric on a pad of newspapers, either on a sturdy table or on the ground.

c Hit the fabric with a hammer until the dye and the image appear

through the cloth. I found that an ordinary household hammer worked well, but I got an even better print by making a pad of kitchen towel and fixing it with a rubber band around the head of the hammer before I began – the paper absorbed the excess dye.

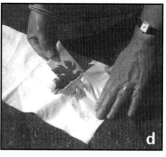

d Take off the tape and remove any crushed remains with a blunt knife.

e Thoroughly dry the fabric, either naturally or – if you can't wait to get on with it – iron it dry (remember to protect your iron with scrap paper). You should now have a beautiful, delicate imprint of your leaf or flower.

FIXING THE IMAGE

Dissolve half a teaspoonful of washing soda in a small amount of hot water, then add this to four pints (2.25 litres) of cold water. Immerse the fabric in the mixture, and leave it soaking for at least six hours or overnight, covered with a plastic sheet or clingfilm.

So that the prints don't discolour each other it's best to lay them flat in the solution, so a flat lasagne-type dish or a cat litter tray is good. (Don't deprive the poor animal: buy a new one for your hammered flowers – they're very useful for dyeing as well.) Alternatively, dip the fabric in the solution then put it flat in a large polythene bag for the same time.

Wash the print thoroughly in detergent to remove any remaining bits of plant matter.

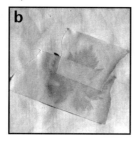

The Basic Boring Bits

If you're an experienced quilter this bit isn't for you, but if you're a beginner this section explains how to do the basics.

ROTARY CUTTING

Rotary cutters speed up fabric cutting, and when accurate strips are essential, as with log cabin, they are invaluable. The cutters are available in large and small sizes, and you need a self-healing mat to cut on and a plastic see-through ruler. You can get mats with measurements marked on them, but I prefer a plain mat combined with a quilters' ruler marked with different measurements.

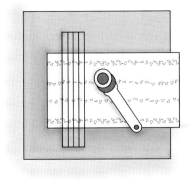

The grain of the fabric must be straight and the selvedge removed so that the fabric won't pull out of alignment while it's being cut. It is possible to cut many layers at once, but for beginners it's easier to do just two at a time. Place the fabric on the mat, put the ruler on top, hold the ruler firmly in place with your left hand, and cut with the cutter blade against the side of the ruler. Cut away from your body with an even movement.

Rotary cutters are very sharp and should be used with care. Always shut the blade after each cut, and keep the cutter well out of the way of small children. You can buy a gadget to re-sharpen the blades: these are useful to have in a quilt group so that people can sharpen the blades at each meeting. If you're keen, you'll find that there are many books devoted entirely to rotary-cut patterns.

MACHINE PIECING

This is obviously the quickest way of joining patchwork pieces. Make sure that you have a good relationship with your machine! Take time to read the instruction book and try out the different things it will do.

Most trouble for patchworkers seems to come with seam allowances. Instructions usually suggest a quarter inch (5mm) seam allowance. Some machines have a special patchwork foot which is marked out with notches at the correct intervals; if you don't have one just gauge it by the width of the foot, and stick to the same foot throughout your project. Another alternative is to measure the correct distance from your needle and stick a strip of masking tape onto the machine to use as a guide.

if you are contributing a block to a group quilt, this is when seam allowances really matter: if you have ever tried to *assemble* a group quilt you will know exactly what I mean!

HAND PIECING

If you don't have a good relationship with your machine, or simply find hand-sewing a relaxing therapy as I do, you can piece accurately by hand. You will need to draw round your template on the back of each patch with a sharp pencil. Before sewing match the drawn lines and pin the pieces vertically to get an accurate join. Sew with running stitches, but with an occasional backstitch to keep it firm. When you get to an edge, leave the seam allowance unstitched so that it can be pressed to either side.

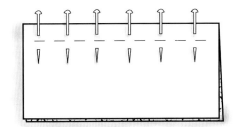

IRONING AND PRESSING

I find a travel iron very useful for small projects; it's also useful to have an iron nearby your machine when you are stitching. A small sleeve-ironing board is handy, or you can make a small board from the cardboard centre of a roll of fabric (smile at your local fabric job assistant); this can be covered in some old flannelette sheet and is useful for taking to classes too.

It's usual to press the seams to the dark side of the work so that they don't show through a light fabric. Sometimes, though, with very thick fabrics you might

---

☞ **TIP**
If you get blood on your quilt, spit on a bit of cloth and rub gently. It removes it better than water.

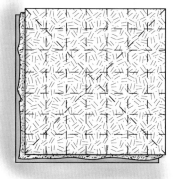

need to press the seams out flat. Occasionally steam ironing can stretch the fabrics: I find that spraying the water from a plastic bottle means you get the dampness just where it's required. (I'm really mean and re-use household cleaner bottles for this.)

MAKING THE QUILT SANDWICH

This isn't a break for a snack! It's the way a quilt is put together. There are three layers: the top, which is usually made from pieced patches; the middle, which is the wadding (this can be polyester or cotton depending on the project or your preference); and the backing, which should be at least 4in (10cm) larger than the top. If your quilt is a bed quilt you will have to join the backing with a seam, or you could use sheeting which is very wide.

The secret of making the sandwich is to get it all flat and not puckered. Depending on the state of your knee joints you can either work on the floor or on a large table: the method is basically the same. OK, so most people don't have large tables and those who do might not want to lend them for tacking quilts on. Either buy a cheap decorating table which folds away and is useful for cutting, then pin half the quilt at a time, or ask the village or church hall if you can use their tables for an hour.

Tape the backing right side down if you're working on a wooden floor or a table: pin it if you're working on a carpet. Make sure that it's nice and taut, then place the wadding (batting, if you're American) on top, smoothing it out. If the wadding needs joining do so by butting the pieces together; don't make a seam, as that would show as a ridge. Place the quilt top right side up on top of the wadding and smooth it well.

If you are hand quilting, tack (baste) the layers together with even tacking stitches, first from corner to corner then from side to side at about 6in (15cm) intervals. This is a laborious job but worth taking time over as it makes the quilting easier and the back smooth if you do it well. There are also tack guns available these days, which shoot little plastic 'stitches' through the layers.

If you are machine quilting, secure the sandwich with safety pins, as the machine will get caught in tacking stitches. You'll need quite a few safety pins; sometimes these can be obtained from dry cleaners' very cheaply. To avoid hurting your fingers and getting blood on your quilt

from your wounds you can close them by pushing the tips onto a tea spoon. When you remove the pins as you machine quilt leave them open; this saves time and effort the next time they are used.

BINDINGS AND BORDERS

This used to be a recurrent problem for me as I always seemed to end up with a wonky-edged quilt! I discovered that it works better if you measure a line through the centre of the quilt and cut each side to that measurement; the sides are then eased or stretched to the same dimension, making the final edge more accurate.

When you're binding a quilt, cut the binding strip twice as wide as required and iron it in half: when it's machined to the quilt edge as shown, it's simple to ease the folded edge over to the back ready for slipstitching in place. An even easier way of binding a quilt is to turn the backing fabric to the front: fold it over in a double fold and slipstitch it to the front. This does of course mean that your backing fabric has to be one that tones with the front of your quilt.

MAKING A CUSHION COVER
For a 12in (30cm) square cover
a Cut the fabric for the backing to 13x16in (33x41cm) and cut this piece in half to make two rectangles 13x8in (33x20.5cm). Fold under and iron a 1in (2.5cm) turning along one long edge of one rectangle, and a 2in (5cm) turning on the other piece.
b Position a 10in (25.5cm) zip under the narrower folded edge and stitch it into place using a zipper foot.
c Position the second piece so that the wider folded edge covers the zip, and machine this into place.
d Open the zip and place the cushion backing face down on the cushion front, right sides together; pin.
e Round the corners evenly; you can do this by drawing round a saucer rim if you're not confident of your curves.

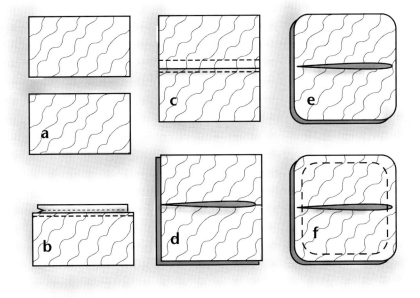

f Machine round the edge and trim the corners. Putting the zip in first is much easier that trying to put it in after the cushion cover is stitched.

EMBROIDERY STITCHES FOR CRAZY PATCHWORK (below)

There are many different stitches that you can use for crazy patchwork, but these are the most common – and some of the most effective.

a Chain stitch

For each link in the chain, insert the needle where the thread emerges and loop the thread around the needle tip. Secure the final link of the chain with a small straight stitch.

b Lazy daisy or detached chain stitch

This stitch consists of individual chain stitches, each one caught down with a small straight stitch.

c French knots

Twist the thread two or three times round the needle, then pull it through to form a knot and take the needle to the back of the work.

d Fly stitch

Bring the needle out on the left of the work, then take it down at the right so that it emerges in a diagonal line as shown. Work a straight stitch vertically to secure each V-shape.

e Feather stitch

Take diagonal stitches alternately to the right and to the left of the stitching line, catching a loop of thread each time as shown.

f Blanket stitch

Create a series of right-angled stitches by putting the needle in vertically as shown. Secure the final loop with a small straight stitch.

g Herringbone stitch

Work from left to right, and take horizontal stitches alternately along the top and bottom of the stitching line to create a criss-cross pattern.

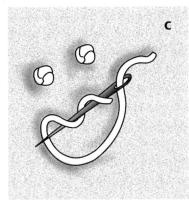
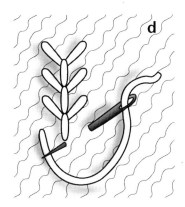
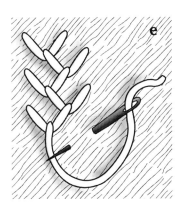
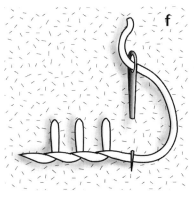
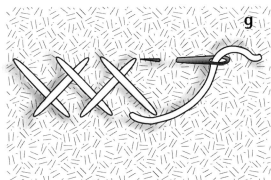

FREEZER PAPER APPLIQUÉ (below)

This is a very accurate form of appliqué which I was first shown years ago on a trip to America. Freezer paper is used there for layering meat in the freezer and is widely available; it's now available in Britain from quilt shops! I've discovered that the glossy paper used to wrap office and photocopy paper works just as well and is free. Make friends with your copy shop assistant!

One side of the paper is slightly waxy and shiny, and when ironed it will stick to fabric temporarily. Draw the pattern onto the non-shiny side and cut out the shape. Cut this shape from fabric, making it slightly larger all round than the freezer paper. Lay the fabric right side down on the ironing board and put the freezer paper glossy side up on top. Clip the edges of the fabric to get a good fit on curves (**a**). Iron the edges down so that they stick and create a neat outline (**b**). Iron the shape down onto your backing fabric and it will stick long enough for you to slipstitch it in place (**c**).

When you have finished your appliqué, turn to the back of the work, cut out the backing fabric inside the stitched shape, very carefully so that you don't cut the front, and remove the paper. With care the shape can be reused a few times and will remain sticky.

FLIP AND SEW (above)

This method is used to cover a piece of foundation fabric with crazy or random piecing. You can trim the patches you add to size as you go, as shown, or leave them ragged at the top and bottom edges and trim them back once all the machining is complete.

a Lay a piece of fabric face down on the previous patch and stitch a straight seam through all layers by machine.

b Fold the new section to the right side and press: it's now ready to have a further patch added on its raw edge.

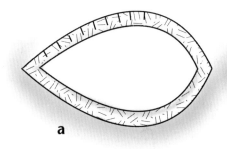

a

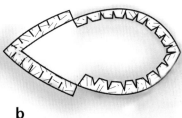

b

c

ᨆ᭄ᨆ ACKNOWLEDGEMENTS ᨆ᭄ᨆ

THANKYOU TO:

Gail and Christopher for their patience and expertise

My family, especially John for putting up with the mess

Paul Stapleton for photography

Zoë and Alice Stapleton for modelling

Linda Tudor for continuing support

Joy and Philip Turton for loan of The Sailor's Return

Ben Bates for loan of his cot quilt

Margaret and Les Jones for loan of the conservatory

Worthing Museum and Art Gallery, for permission to reproduce the photograph on page 6

STOCKISTS:

The Quilt Room, 20 West Street, Dorking, Surrey RH4 1BL

Crafty Ribbons, 3 Beechwood, Tin Pot Lane, Blandford, Dorset DT11 7TS

Lady Sew And Sew, 69 St Andrews Road, Henley on Thames, Oxon RG9 1PG

Sunflower Fabrics, 139 Castle Road, Bedford MK40 3RS

Ribbon Designs, PO Box 382, Edgware, Middlesex HA8 7RU

Higgledy Piggledy Patchwork, 26 Carr Field Drive, Luddenham, Halifax, West Yorkshire HX2 6RJ